The 90-Day Rewire

The 90-Day Rewire

Matthew Petchinsky

1

The 90-Day Rewire: Transform Your Neural Pathways Before Spring Blooms

By: Matthew Petchinsky

Disclaimer

*This book is for educational and inspirational use only. It is not a substitute for professional medical, financial, psychological, or therapeutic advice. The practices, exercises, and insights presented throughout **The 90-Day Rewire – Transform Your Neural Pathways Before Spring Blooms** are designed to encourage self-reflection, personal growth, and improved daily habits, but they are not intended to diagnose, treat, cure, or prevent any condition.*

Neuroscience-inspired strategies, mindset techniques, and behavioral adjustments discussed in this book are offered as general informational tools. Every individual's neurological, emotional, physical, and financial circumstances are unique, and results may vary. **Always consult with licensed medical professionals, mental health practitioners, or financial advisors** before beginning any new health regimen, mental wellness practice, or lifestyle change—especially if you have pre-existing medical conditions, psychological concerns, or financial vulnerabilities.

The author and publisher are not liable for any damages, losses, or consequences arising from the application or misapplication of the concepts within this text. **Use your discernment, move at your own pace, and seek professional support when needed.**

This book is meant to empower, not replace expert guidance.

Introduction

You can't plant new crops in old soil.

If you want a different year, a different outcome, and a different version of yourself by the time spring arrives, you must begin by tending to the ground beneath everything you think, feel, and do: your neural pathways.

Most people try to change their life by adding more—more goals, more tasks, more pressure, more expectations. But transformation doesn't begin with addition. It begins with subtraction. It begins with pruning. Just as a gardener clears away last season's debris before planting anything new, you must identify and remove the mental weeds that have taken root: outdated beliefs, stress patterns, emotional loops, and survival habits that once protected you but now hold you back.

The next ninety days are not about forcing yourself into discipline or willpower warfare. They are about creating *conditions* for clarity, motivation, and new identity wiring to grow. Recent neuroscience confirms that the brain remains malleable—capable of reshaping itself through focused repetition, emotional engagement, and strategic cognitive disruption. In other words: **you can literally rebuild your brain's wiring in three months.**

This book is your structured, science-informed blueprint for doing exactly that.

During this 90-day process, you will learn how to nudge your brain out of autopilot, challenge worn-out neural patterns, and plant new circuits of motivation, resilience, and intentional living. You will engage in micro-practices that stimulate neuroplasticity, rituals that support emotional regulation, and weekly rewiring frameworks that help you understand why you think the way you do—and how to change it.

You'll also discover the secret power of timing. Winter's quiet, stillness, and introspection create the perfect environment for inner reconstruction. Before the world begins to thaw and bloom, you will already be ahead: calibrated, rewired, and aligned with the identity you want to step into when spring arrives.

Whether you are healing old patterns, building new habits, sharpening your focus, strengthening your mindset, or preparing for a life pivot, **The 90-Day Rewire** gives you the tools to do it at the neural level—not with surface-level motivation, but with deep cognitive redesign.

This is not self-help fluff. This is not wishful thinking.

This is a method.

A seasonal reset.

A neural renovation.

A reclaiming of who you can become when the mind is finally ready to support the life you've been trying to build.

Turn the page.

Let's start clearing the soil.

New growth is waiting.

Chapter 1: Neuroplastic Beginnings – Understanding Your Brain's Adaptive Power

The Brain That Never Stops Changing

Your brain is not a fixed machine—it is a living ecosystem of thoughts, emotions, chemical signals, habits, and memories. Even when you believe nothing is happening, your mind is constantly editing, reinforcing, and updating neural pathways based on what you repeatedly think, feel, and do. This dynamic quality is known as **neuroplasticity**, and it is one of the most powerful biological gifts you have. It means you are never stuck, never finished, and never limited to the patterns that shaped your past.

For decades, scientists believed the adult brain was static. We now know the opposite is true: your brain is always reshaping itself, pruning old connections and building new ones—just like a garden. This is why change is possible even after years of repetition, trauma, or stagnation. The moment you introduce new behaviors, thoughts, and emotional experiences, the brain begins reorganizing its circuitry. Neuroplasticity is not a rare event; it is an everyday phenomenon.

Understanding this is liberating because it shifts the narrative from "this is just how I am" to "this is how I am today." Who you become in the future depends on what you spark, nurture, and practice now. The mind's architecture bends to your repeated choices. Every intentional thought is a seed. Every habit is a root. Every emotional shift is sunlight or rain.

Recognizing your adaptive power is the first step in this 90-day journey. Before new neural pathways grow, you must believe they can. Your biology is on your side. Your mind is programmable, responsive, and always ready to evolve—even if change has felt slow or impossible until now.

Neural Pathways: Highways of Habit

Neural pathways are the interconnected routes your brain uses to transmit information. The more you use a pathway—whether it's a thought, reaction, or behavior—the stronger and faster it becomes. This is why some habits feel automatic: you've built a neurological superhighway. Conversely, pathways you rarely use weaken, shrink, and eventually fade, like abandoned roads overtaken by weeds.

This is the basis of both empowerment and self-sabotage. When you repeatedly think "I'll never change," that belief becomes a reinforced circuit. When you repeatedly choose avoidance over action, the avoidance pathway becomes dominant. But the good news is that these pathways are not permanent. You can deactivate old ones through disuse and grow new ones through intentional repetition.

Every time you interrupt an old habit—even briefly—you begin weakening its neural grip. Every time you choose a new behavior—even awkwardly—you begin laying down the first wiring of a fresh pathway. Small changes matter because the brain responds to consistency, not intensity.

In this chapter, you will learn how to consciously dismantle unhelpful neural highways and start constructing ones that support your future identity. Think of it as rebuilding your internal transportation system: slow at first, unstoppable over time.

Identity Wiring: Why "Who You Are" Is a Neural Pattern

Most people believe personality is a fixed trait, but neuroscience reveals that identity is largely a collection of reinforced neural patterns. "I'm bad with money," "I can't focus," "I always panic," or "I never finish anything" are not personal truths—they are learned patterns of wiring strengthened over many years. Identity is malleable because the brain continually updates itself based on behavior repetition.

When you behave in alignment with an identity—even unintentionally—the brain marks it as familiar and reduces resistance. This is how identities become comfortable even when they are painful. A habit may harm you, but if it's neurologically familiar, your brain treats it as safe. This is why change feels threatening: you are not fighting your willpower, you are challenging your wiring.

To rewrite identity, you must deliberately engage in behaviors that align with your desired self. When repeated, these behaviors create new circuitry that eventually becomes the "default you." This takes time, consistency, and emotional engagement—the three key drivers of neural transformation.

Your identity is not who you were yesterday; it is who you repeatedly choose to be today. With each shift in thought or action, you sculpt a new version of yourself at the cellular level.

Emotional Plasticity: How Feelings Reshape the Mind

Emotions are not just psychological—they are neurochemical events that imprint deeply on the brain. High emotional intensity strengthens whatever circuitry is active in that moment. This is why traumatic experiences create strong neural footprints—and why powerful positive experiences can accelerate rewiring.

When you attach emotion to a new habit, the brain flags it as important and prioritizes building the related pathway. This is why enthusiasm amplifies learning and why boredom slows it. Emotional plasticity means that how you feel while adopting changes directly influences how quickly your brain rewires.

Recognizing this gives you a strategic advantage. If you pair new habits with positive emotions—celebration, gratitude, pride, excitement—you help your brain encode them faster. Conversely, if you repeatedly pair stress or fear with a new habit, the brain may reject the change because it associates it with discomfort.

This chapter will teach you how to regulate emotions strategically so your neural rewiring becomes smoother, faster, and more sustainable.

Cognitive Pruning: Clearing Old Mental Weeds

Neuroplasticity is not only about growth; it is also about removal. The brain prunes unused pathways, just as a gardener trims dead branches to help new growth thrive. When a thought pattern or habit stops receiving attention, the brain gradually dissolves the neural connections supporting it.

This is why awareness and interruption are critical steps in change. You cannot create new wiring on top of clutter. You must first identify the thoughts, reactions, and beliefs that no longer serve your growth. These are your mental weeds: old coping strategies, outdated fears, inherited narratives, and autopilot responses that once protected you but now limit your potential.

Pruning does not happen overnight. It requires conscious disengagement—catching yourself in old patterns and choosing not to follow them. Even if you slip sometimes, the repeated act of interruption weakens old circuitry.

The next chapters will guide you through strategic pruning cycles that prepare your mind for entirely new neural conditions—fertile ground for the identity you're building.

Neurochemistry 101: The Chemicals of Change

Your thoughts and habits do not exist in isolation—they influence and are influenced by neurochemicals such as dopamine, serotonin, norepinephrine, and GABA. These chemicals regulate mood, motivation, focus, and resilience. Understanding their roles helps you work with your biology instead of against it.

Dopamine drives reward and anticipation. It spikes when you pursue goals and builds momentum for new habits. Serotonin stabilizes mood and confidence, making change feel secure. Norepinephrine amplifies focus and alertness, especially during moments of challenge. GABA calms the nervous system, allowing new behaviors to embed without overwhelming stress.

When neurochemicals are balanced, habit formation accelerates. When imbalanced—due to stress, poor sleep, or emotional overload—rewiring becomes difficult. This is why you may intellectually want to change but feel physically unable.

By aligning your lifestyle habits (sleep, hydration, micro-movements, breaks, emotional regulation) with your rewiring goals, you create a chemical environment that supports transformation. Think of this as preparing the internal soil before planting new seeds.

The Habit Loop and the Brain's Resistance to Change

Every habit consists of a cue, routine, and reward. When you repeat this loop, the brain memorizes it and begins automating it to save energy. Automation is helpful for positive habits—but destructive for negative ones. This automation is why you sometimes act automatically before you even realize what you're doing.

The brain is not trying to sabotage you—it is trying to conserve resources. New behaviors require significantly more energy than old ones, so the brain initially resists change. This resistance feels like procrastination, anxiety, discomfort, or self-doubt.

Understanding this resistance allows you to anticipate it instead of interpreting it as failure. When resistance appears, it is not a sign to stop—it is a sign that new wiring is forming. The brain is adjusting to a new loop, and with repetition, the discomfort subsides as the new routine becomes automatic.

This chapter will teach you techniques to dismantle old habit loops and engineer new ones that align with your desired identity.

Neuroplastic Windows: Your Brain's Best Times for Change

The brain has periods of heightened plasticity—windows when rewiring is faster and easier. These windows occur when you are emotionally activated, learning something new, shifting environments, or experiencing transitions. Seasonal changes, like the shift from winter to spring, naturally increase neuroplasticity due to shifts in light, mood, and circadian rhythms.

Understanding when your brain is most receptive to rewiring helps you accelerate transformation. Morning hours, moments after exercise, and periods following emotional breakthroughs are especially potent plasticity windows. These are ideal times for affirmations, habit installation, and identity reinforcement.

When you take advantage of these windows, you reinforce new pathways more efficiently. When you ignore them, change becomes slower and more draining. The goal of this 90-day journey is to intentionally align your behaviors with your brain's natural cycles of adaptability.

You will learn to recognize these windows and use them deliberately to fast-track your growth.

The Role of Attention: What You Focus On, You Strengthen

Attention is one of the most powerful forces in neuroplasticity. What you repeatedly focus on becomes neurologically reinforced—whether helpful or harmful. This means dwelling on fears strengthens fear circuits, while focusing on solutions strengthens resilience circuits.

You cannot eliminate all negative thoughts, but you can consciously shift which ones you nurture. When you redirect attention, you redirect wiring. This process requires patience because the brain loves familiar patterns and will attempt to return to them.

Over time, however, your attention becomes a spotlight that signals the brain where to build highways and where to let pathways die out. This is why mindfulness, reflection, and identity-based affirmations are core components of neural rewiring. They shape the architecture of your thought patterns from the inside out.

This chapter will teach you how to use attention strategically so that your mind builds the circuits that support your future instead of your past.

Breaking Neural Autopilot

Autopilot is the enemy of transformation. It is the brain's default mode network, responsible for repeating familiar thoughts and behaviors without conscious input. Autopilot keeps you predictable, but it also keeps you stuck. When you act without awareness, you reinforce old pathways—no matter how badly you want to change.

The first step in breaking autopilot is recognition. Notice when your brain slips into old loops: scrolling when anxious, procrastinating when overwhelmed, or repeating narratives from your past. These moments are opportunities to choose differently and disrupt the neural script.

Even small interruptions create powerful openings in the neural structure. A pause, a deep breath, or a single new action stops the autopilot system long enough for you to redirect behavior. Over time, these micro-interruptions weaken old pathways and strengthen new ones.

This chapter equips you with techniques for interrupting autopilot and replacing it with conscious, intentional behavior.

Neuroplasticity and the Seasons of Your Life

Every life phase comes with different emotional climates, responsibilities, and internal needs. Your neural wiring adapts to these phases, which is why you behave differently at different ages or during major transitions. Understanding how seasons of life influence your neural design allows you to approach change with compassion and strategy.

During stressful seasons, the brain strengthens survival pathways. During calm seasons, it strengthens learning pathways. During transitional seasons—like the 90 days leading into spring—the brain becomes highly receptive to identity shifts because environmental and behavioral cues naturally change.

When you align personal reinvention with seasonal neuroplastic patterns, change becomes smoother. You feel less resistance, more curiosity, and more momentum. This is why this 90-day period was chosen: it matches your brain's natural seasonal shift toward activation, clarity, and renewal.

Recognizing your internal seasons empowers you to work with your biology instead of forcing yourself against it.

Preparing the Mind for Rewiring

Before you begin reshaping neural pathways, you must create the right internal conditions: calm, clarity, intention, and emotional openness. The brain cannot rewire under chronic stress or emotional chaos. This is why grounding techniques, rituals of reflection, and micro-lifestyle shifts are essential.

Preparing the mind means reducing noise—both internal and external. It means clearing old beliefs, adjusting your self-talk, and establishing a supportive internal narrative. It also means creating physical and emotional environments that reduce friction and support new habits.

Without preparation, change feels like pushing through mud. With preparation, change becomes a natural unfolding. This chapter lays the foundation for mental readiness so your rewiring is efficient, sustainable, and aligned with who you want to become.

Your next 90 days will be different because you are not building change on top of chaos; you are building it on intentionality.

20 Lessons from Chapter 1

1. Your brain is always changing—never static.
2. Thoughts and habits become stronger through repetition.
3. Identity is a collection of reinforced neural patterns.
4. Emotional intensity accelerates neural imprinting.
5. Old pathways weaken through lack of use.
6. New pathways grow through deliberate repetition.
7. Neurochemicals influence your ability to change.
8. The brain resists change to conserve energy.
9. Awareness interrupts neural autopilot.
10. Seasonal shifts increase neuroplastic sensitivity.
11. Attention functions as a spotlight that shapes wiring.
12. Interrupting old habits weakens their circuits.
13. Positive emotion attached to habits accelerates learning.
14. Familiar patterns feel "safe" even when harmful.
15. The brain thrives on consistency, not intensity.
16. Identity change requires behavior change first.
17. Neural pruning is essential for mental clarity.
18. Focused repetition is the engine of transformation.
19. Morning and post-movement windows boost plasticity.
20. Mind preparation is the foundation of rewiring.

Exercises:

Exercise 1: Neural Awareness Scan

Spend 10 minutes noticing your most repeated thoughts and behaviors today.
Mark them as:
• Helpful
• Neutral
• Harmful
This scan begins your pruning process.

Exercise 2: Pattern Interruption Ritual

Choose one harmful habit (overthinking, avoidance, scrolling, self-criticism).
For the next 7 days, interrupt it *once per day* with a different action.
Each interruption is a neural dismantling.

Exercise 3: Identity Seed Statement

Write a single sentence that represents the identity you want to become in 90 days.
Repeat it once every morning and once each night to begin laying new neural roots.

10 Journal Prompts

1. What old thought loops do I repeat most often, and how do they shape my behavior?
2. What identity am I unintentionally reinforcing through my current habits?
3. Which neural pathways feel the strongest in my life—and why?
4. When does my brain feel most resistant to change?
5. What beliefs am I ready to prune or release?
6. What new habits do I want my brain to automate by spring?
7. How do my emotional states influence my decisions?
8. Where am I still acting on autopilot?
9. What identity do I want to be known for in 90 days?
10. How can I support my neurochemistry through lifestyle changes?

Closing Reflection

Your brain is not a fixed monument—it is a living landscape. Every thought plants a seed, every emotion waters a garden, and every habit sculpts the terrain. As you close this chapter, recognize that you hold the tools to transform your inner architecture. Nothing about your wiring is permanent; it is waiting for your instruction. These next 90 days are not only about learning new habits—they are about becoming the gardener of your mind, pruning the old, nurturing the new, and cultivating a version of yourself ready to bloom with the spring.

Chapter 2: Pattern Interrupts – Breaking Loops That Sabotage Growth

Understanding the Loop: How Patterns Become Psychological Traps

Every self-sabotaging pattern begins as a learned response—something you repeated enough times for the brain to encode it as "the safest, quickest option." Loops form around stress, fear, discomfort, or uncertainty. When you encounter a trigger, the brain runs its familiar cycle: cue → reaction → reward. Even harmful behaviors deliver a perceived reward, such as relief, distraction, numbness, or escape.

Over time, these loops become so automatic that you stop noticing them. They activate faster than conscious thought, often within milliseconds. Before you know it, you've fallen into the same reaction, the same shutdown, the same anxiety burst, or the same avoidance behavior. The trap is not the behavior itself—it is the *timing*. The loop activates faster than your awareness.

To break a loop, you must interrupt it *before* it finishes. That requires recognizing its earliest signals. Every loop has a beginning, even if it feels instant. A sensation in your stomach. A tightening in your chest. A mental script starting to replay. These micro-signals are your entry points.

Pattern interrupts work because they break this invisible chain. Even a tiny disruption weakens the neural sequence and introduces new wiring possibilities. Learning these interruptions is the key to dismantling sabotaging cycles from the inside out.

The Anatomy of a Self-Sabotaging Habit

Self-sabotage is not irrational—it is adaptive. Your survival brain prioritizes familiarity over progress because familiar patterns require the least energy and feel the safest. That means patterns like procrastination, overthinking, emotional withdrawal, or impulsive reactions are often misguided attempts to protect you from threat.

These habits follow a predictable structure. First, a trigger (stress, criticism, uncertainty). Then the internal cue (fear spike, racing heart, negative self-talk). Next comes the automatic behavior (shutdown, distraction, anger, avoidance). Finally, the reward (temporary relief). The brain, recognizing the relief, strengthens the loop.

Understanding this structure demystifies self-sabotage. You are not weak or flawed—you are neurologically efficient. But efficiency must be redirected toward growth rather than survival patterns that no longer serve you.

Once you understand the anatomy of your own sabotaging cycles, you can begin breaking them piece by piece. Pattern interrupts help you target the exact moment the loop forms and replace old behaviors with conscious choices.

Micro-Interrupts: The Small Shifts That Start Big Change

A micro-interrupt is a small action that disrupts an automatic loop before it completes. It is not about willpower—it's about destabilizing the circuit long enough to re-route it. Even a five-second pause can weaken deeply ingrained habits because it forces the brain to switch from autopilot to awareness.

Micro-interrupts can be physical (changing posture), cognitive (asking yourself a question), or emotional (taking a grounding breath). What matters is timing. The earlier the interrupt, the more powerful its rewiring effect. A micro-interrupt at the beginning of a loop is like pulling a weed by its root; a late interrupt is like trimming the leaves.

Over time, micro-interrupts accumulate. They signal to your brain that the old loop is no longer the default. Eventually, the loop collapses from lack of consistency, and the brain begins forming new pathways aligned with your intentional actions.

These interruptions may feel strange or insignificant at first, but they are the building blocks of your new identity wiring. Consistency creates transformation—even in moments that last only seconds.

Breaking Emotional Loops Before They Hijack You

Emotional loops form when a feeling triggers a familiar reaction—panic, shutdown, anger, withdrawal—before you consciously interpret the situation. These loops are fast because they originate in the amygdala, the part of your brain wired for rapid survival decisions.

Interrupting emotional loops begins with intercepting the feeling before it becomes a reaction. This requires attunement to your body, because emotions often show up physically before mentally. A tight jaw, rapid heartbeat, shakiness, or heat rising in your chest are early signals.

By interrupting the loop at the physical stage—before the cognitive story forms—you weaken the emotional autopilot. Grounding breaths, slow movement, or naming the emotion aloud disrupt its momentum. These tools stabilize neurochemical spikes and bring the thinking brain back online.

Over time, emotional pattern interrupts transform reactivity into responsiveness. You stop being hijacked by feelings and start navigating them with clarity and intention.

Cognitive Interrupts: Stopping Thought Spirals

Thought spirals—rumination, overthinking, catastrophizing—are cognitive loops that drain mental energy. They are triggered by uncertainty, fear, or unmet expectations, and once activated, they pull you into deeper levels of anxiety or self-doubt.

A cognitive interrupt does not aim to suppress the thought—it aims to shift the brain's focus. Thoughts thrive on attention. When you redirect attention, the neural circuit loses reinforcement. Techniques like asking a grounding question ("What is within my control right now?"), naming the spiral ("This is my overthinking loop"), or shifting sensory focus can stop the mental spiral before it accelerates.

Interrupting thought patterns breaks their intensity. Once the loop weakens, you can introduce alternative thinking patterns that support your future identity rather than reinforce old fears.

Cognitive interrupts rebuild mental clarity by dissolving the mental scripts that have kept you stuck in repetitive cycles.

Behavioral Interrupts: Disrupting Physical Autopilot

Many sabotaging habits—scrolling, snacking, pacing, isolating—are behavioral loops triggered by emotional discomfort. You don't choose them consciously; your body performs them automatically because the neural pathways are deeply grooved.

Behavioral interrupts involve injecting a new physical action when the urge arises. Even something as small as standing up, stretching, changing rooms, or placing your phone face-down disrupts the neural sequence. These changes force the brain to pause and reassess, breaking the automatic momentum.

Behavioral interrupts also create space for conscious choice. Once the automatic behavior is interrupted, you can select a new action that reflects your desired identity.

The more frequently you interrupt an unwanted behavior, the faster your brain dissolves the old neural loop and replaces it with a new one aligned with your goals.

The 5-Second Neuroplastic Rule

One of the most powerful tools in pattern interruption is the five-second rule: if you interrupt a loop within five seconds of the urge, you prevent the brain from completing the sequence. This rule works because neural loops require uninterrupted momentum. A brief delay halts dopamine release and stops the cycle from strengthening.

To use the rule, catch the moment just before the old habit begins. Count backwards: **5–4–3–2–1**, and then take a new action. The countdown activates the prefrontal cortex—the logical brain—and temporarily shuts down autopilot.

This technique is effective for procrastination, fear-based avoidance, emotional suppression, compulsive behaviors, and negative self-talk. Over time, using the five-second interrupt weakens the old patterns and reinforces your new identity.

Each time you count down, you are practicing neural leadership—training your brain to follow your instruction rather than old wiring.

Choosing the "Next Best Action" Instead of Perfection

Perfectionism is one of the biggest saboteurs of neural change. The belief that you must act perfectly or completely often prevents you from acting at all. This creates a loop of hesitation → paralysis → shame → avoidance, which reinforces the belief that change is difficult.

Pattern interrupts thrive on simplicity. You do not need to complete a task—you just need to choose the next best action. One step disrupts the paralysis loop. One shift breaks the mental blockage. One tiny movement begins rewiring your identity.

Once the brain sees progress, dopamine releases, and the loop shifts from avoidance to momentum. The next best action is not just a productivity tool—it is a neurological strategy that teaches your brain to move through fear and uncertainty.

This principle builds sustainable growth and ensures that your rewiring journey is based on consistency rather than pressure.

Loop Identification: Mapping Your Personal Sabotage Cycles

To break sabotaging loops, you must first identify them clearly. Most loops run beneath conscious awareness, triggered so rapidly that you only recognize them after they have caused damage—lost time, emotional overload, avoidance, or self-criticism.

Mapping your loops involves identifying their cues, triggers, sensations, thoughts, and behaviors. This awareness creates an internal map that makes the once-invisible visible. You begin noticing patterns you previously dismissed as “just how I am.”

Mapping your loops is not about judgment; it is about data collection. The more precise your mapping, the more surgical your pattern interrupts become. Instead of blindly battling habits, you target them at their roots.

Clarity gives you power. Once you understand your loop structure, breaking it becomes a strategic act rather than a struggle.

The Science of Interruption: Why Disruption Weakens Neural Strength

Pattern interrupts work because they introduce unpredictability into the brain's automated pathways. Neural circuits depend on repetition to stay strong. When you disrupt a pattern, even slightly, the brain can't predict the next step—and unpredictability is kryptonite to old circuits.

Each interruption weakens the pathway through synaptic pruning. The brain gradually dissolves connections that are inconsistent or rarely used. Over time, this reduces the intensity of urges, emotional reactions, and cognitive spirals.

Simultaneously, interruptions strengthen new neural pathways. When you replace an old habit with a new action—even a small one—you create a fresh circuit. Repetition wires it in.

This dual process—weakening old wiring while building new wiring—is the foundation of identity transformation.

Replacing Loops with Identity-Based Patterns

A pattern interrupt is only half of the process. After breaking a loop, you must replace it with a behavior aligned with your future identity. Otherwise, the brain defaults back to old habits.

Identity-based patterns are actions that reflect who you want to become. For example:

- Instead of avoidance → take a 2-minute action.
- Instead of overthinking → choose a grounding question.
- Instead of emotional shutdown → name the feeling.
- Instead of procrastination → complete one micro-task.

Replacing loops ensures that the brain has something new to wire. Without replacement, interruptions feel chaotic and short-lived. With replacement, they become transformational.

Your desired identity becomes the source code for your new neural patterns.

Building a Lifestyle of Interrupts

Pattern interruptions are not one-time events—they become a lifestyle. A way of living awake rather than asleep. A method of choosing intention over autopilot. Over time, interrupts become second nature, and you begin catching loops before they even form.

A lifestyle of interrupts means you live with awareness. You recognize triggers without collapsing into them. You pause before reacting. You choose actions that support your identity rather than sabotage it. This creates a neural environment of empowerment rather than reactivity.

Living in this way reshapes your entire internal landscape. Suddenly, habits you struggled with for years dissolve. Loops that controlled your days disappear. Motivation becomes natural rather than forced.

When interruptions become habitual, you transform your mind at its roots.

20 Lessons from Chapter 2

1. Self-sabotage is a learned loop, not a personal flaw.
2. All loops have triggers, cues, reactions, and rewards.
3. Pattern interrupts succeed by disrupting the sequence early.
4. Emotional loops are fastest due to amygdala activation.
5. Physical sensations are early signals of emotional loops.
6. Cognitive interrupts redirect attention away from spirals.
7. Behavioral interrupts break automatic physical reactions.
8. Micro-interrupts are small but powerful.
9. The five-second rule activates conscious control.
10. Interrupting loops weakens their neural strength.
11. Replacement behaviors are essential for rewiring.
12. Awareness precedes interruption.
13. Familiarity—not logic—creates sabotaging habits.
14. The brain resists change because it prefers efficiency.
15. Identifying loops reveals unconscious patterns.
16. Perfectionism often triggers sabotage loops.
17. Interrupts create neurochemical shifts in your favor.
18. A single interrupt can prevent hours of sabotage.
19. Repetition of interrupts builds new identity pathways.
20. Living with awareness creates long-term transformation.

Exercises:

Exercise 1: Loop Mapping Worksheet

Write down one pattern you want to break.

Identify:

- Trigger
- First physical cue
- First thought
- Automatic behavior
- Reward

This becomes your neural map.

Exercise 2: 5-Second Interrupt Drill

For the next 3 days, when an urge to fall into an old loop arises, count **5–4–3–2–1** and take a new action immediately.

Exercise 3: Replacement Action Plan

Choose one new identity-based action to replace your old loop. Practice inserting it after every interrupt this week.

10 Journal Prompts

1. What sabotaging loops do I repeat most often?
2. What triggers activate these loops?
3. What physical cues show up before the pattern starts?
4. What thoughts usually accompany the loop?
5. What emotional rewards do I get from the loop?
6. How would my future identity respond instead?
7. What is one tiny interrupt I can practice today?
8. Which loop has caused the most long-term damage in my life?
9. How can I build awareness to catch loops earlier?
10. What new identity-based patterns do I want to install?

Closing Reflection

Interrupting your patterns is an act of reclaiming your mind from old programming. Every interruption is a moment of clarity, a moment of power, a moment where your future self steps into the present and takes the lead. You are not fighting against your brain—you are teaching it a new way to live. In breaking these loops, you create new possibilities. You build pathways that carry you toward who you're becoming. Each interrupt is a spark of transformation, and over these next 90 days, these sparks will grow into a fire that shapes a stronger, clearer, more intentional you.

Chapter 3: The Wiring Blueprint – Installing New Cognitive Behaviors

The Architecture of Behavioral Design

Every new cognitive behavior begins with a blueprint—a mental design that tells your brain what to build, how to build it, and where it fits within your identity. Without a blueprint, new habits collapse under the weight of uncertainty. With one, the brain receives a clear set of instructions, making change predictable and sustainable.

Your cognitive blueprint is not just a list of habits—it is a system. It includes triggers, emotional anchors, physical cues, environment shifts, and identity alignment. When these elements work together, the brain adopts the new behavior with far less resistance. Neuroscience shows that structured behaviors are encoded faster because the brain thrives on clarity and repetition.

Designing a behavioral blueprint allows you to shift from reactive living to intentional living. Instead of relying on motivation, you rely on structure—the kind your brain can automate over time.

The rest of this chapter shows you how to create that structure so new behaviors have a strong foundation and can grow into automatic patterns that support your future identity.

Installing Neural Foundations: Small Behaviors, Big Wiring

The brain doesn't build new wiring from dramatic change—it builds from small, consistent actions repeated enough times to become familiar. Small behaviors reduce resistance because they require minimal energy, which encourages the brain to accept them without triggering survival mechanisms.

These micro-behaviors may seem insignificant, but they create the first trench of a new neural pathway. Once the trench is dug, repetition deepens it. With time, the pathway becomes a road, then a highway, then the primary route your brain uses automatically.

This is why cognitive installation begins with the smallest possible version of the habit you want. Not the whole workout—just the shoes. Not the whole project—just the first two minutes. Not the entire behavior—just the activation step. Once installed, the brain builds momentum.

Never underestimate the power of small. Small is the structure. Small is the start. Small is the spark that grows into rewired identity.

The Power of Consistency Cues

A consistency cue is a signal that tells your brain, "This behavior matters." It could be a sound (a morning alarm), a location (a dedicated work spot), a visual cue (a journal on your desk), or a ritual (a deep breath before starting). These cues activate neural readiness by linking the behavior to a repeated trigger.

The more consistently the cue appears, the faster the brain encodes the behavior. Over time, the cue alone becomes enough to activate the behavioral circuit—like Pavlov's bell but directed toward your success.

Consistency cues also reduce friction. Instead of relying on willpower, you leverage triggers your brain already recognizes. This creates fluid behavior installation, removing the strain of decision-making and reducing emotional resistance.

Every new behavior needs at least one cue. Without it, the brain lacks a reliable spark to activate the behavior consistently.

Strategic Repetition: How Behaviors Become Neural Highways

Repetition is the engine of neuroplasticity. The more often a behavior is repeated, the more signals travel across the same neural pathway. Over time, the pathway becomes insulated, making it faster, stronger, and more efficient. This is the neurological process of myelination.

But repetition must be strategic. Random practice doesn't produce strong wiring—consistent repetition in the same context does. This is because the brain pairs behaviors with environmental and emotional cues. Repeating a habit in the same place, around the same time, under similar conditions accelerates encoding.

Strategic repetition creates reliability. The brain learns: "This is who we are now." Once the habit becomes self-identity, it no longer requires effort.

Consistency rewires the brain. Identity locks it in.

Momentum Loops: Fueling Your New Behaviors

Momentum loops are behavioral sequences that create forward movement. Unlike sabotaging loops, which trigger regression, momentum loops generate progress. They begin with a small action that produces a sense of accomplishment. That feeling releases dopamine, which reinforces the action and makes it easier to repeat.

Momentum loops can be engineered intentionally. By breaking a behavior into small steps and completing the easiest one first, you activate a dopamine cycle that carries you into the harder steps. This approach sidesteps procrastination and emotional blocks.

When used consistently, momentum loops transform how you approach goals. You stop relying on motivation and begin relying on structured momentum—a reliable neurological fuel source.

This blueprint helps you build a life where doors open because you nudged them open, not because you waited for inspiration to strike.

Identity Encoding: Behaviors that Shape Who You Become

Identity encoding is the process by which behaviors reshape your sense of self. You cannot simply "think" your way into a new identity—you must behave your way into it. Each action becomes a vote toward who you believe you are becoming.

When you act in alignment with a future version of yourself, the brain notices. It updates your internal identity files. Over time, the old identity weakens from disuse, and the new identity strengthens through repetition and emotion.

Identity encoding makes change permanent. Instead of saying "I'm trying to become...," you shift to "I am someone who...," and the brain begins adopting that as truth.

This chapter teaches you how to intentionally install identity-based cognitive behaviors that align with the transformation you are shaping.

Environment as a Wiring Tool

Your environment is not neutral—it either supports or sabotages your rewiring. The brain is deeply responsive to environmental cues, even ones you don't consciously notice. Messy spaces increase stress. Tidy spaces increase focus. Distracting spaces reduce consistency. Minimal spaces reduce cognitive friction.

To install new behaviors, redesign your environment so your desired behaviors are easy and your old behaviors are inconvenient. This is called "environmental sculpting," and it is one of the fastest ways to rewire habits because it eliminates decision fatigue.

For example, if you want to write daily, keep the journal open. If you want to hydrate more, keep water within reach. If you want to stop scrolling, leave the phone across the room. These small shifts create neurological support beams for your new habits.

Your environment becomes part of your blueprint—an external extension of your internal transformation.

The Role of Clarity in Cognitive Installation

The brain cannot install vague behaviors. “Be healthier” or “be more focused” are too abstract for neural encoding. Behaviors must be specific, measurable, and emotionally relevant. Clarity helps the brain understand the blueprint and reduces resistance rooted in ambiguity.

When behaviors have clarity, the brain can predict the sequence and execute it smoothly. When behaviors are unclear, the brain hesitates, triggering avoidance loops and emotional discomfort.

Clarity eliminates confusion, and confusion is one of the biggest barriers to rewiring. The clearer the behavior, the faster the installation.

Your wiring blueprint must be precise if you want long-term, automated cognitive change.

Emotional Anchoring: Wiring Behaviors with Feeling

Emotion accelerates neural installation. When you attach an emotion—pride, relief, excitement—to a new behavior, the brain marks it as meaningful and strengthens the pathway. This is because emotional experiences trigger stronger neurochemical responses, which accelerate encoding.

To install new behaviors faster, you must consciously attach meaning to them. Celebrate small victories. Take pride in micro-progress. Reward yourself for consistency. These emotional anchors tell the brain, "This matters. Keep building."

Without emotional anchoring, behaviors remain purely mechanical and take longer to become part of your identity. With anchoring, behaviors become deeply personal and neurologically prioritized.

Your wiring blueprint must include emotional reinforcement to ensure your new patterns thrive.

Cognitive Sequencing: Building Behaviors in Layers

The brain wires new behaviors best when they are built in layers. Trying to install multiple behaviors at once overwhelms the prefrontal cortex and triggers resistance. But sequencing behaviors—installing one at a time—creates stability and structure.

Start with foundational behaviors: sleep, hydration, environment, micro-actions. Once these become stable, add the next layer—productivity, emotional regulation, focus skills. After that, install identity-based cognitive behaviors that reflect your long-term transformation.

Layering ensures your brain is not overburdened. Instead of chaotic rewiring, you get structured growth—like building floors on a skyscraper.

Sustainable transformation requires sequencing. This is how your new identity is built safely and powerfully.

Habit Stacking: Linking New Patterns to Old Ones

Habit stacking is one of the most efficient cognitive installation methods. It involves linking a new behavior to an existing one so the brain adopts it as a natural extension of a familiar routine. Because the old habit is already wired, the new habit gains traction from the connection.

For example:

- After brushing your teeth → repeat your identity statement.
- After making your bed → review your top priority.
- After pouring morning water → do one minute of breathing.
- After finishing work → write your next-day plan.

Habit stacking piggybacks new behaviors onto existing neural pathways, reducing friction and accelerating coding.

Your blueprint will be incomplete without stacking—it is one of the most powerful rewiring tools available.

Automation: When New Behaviors Become Who You Are

The final stage of behavioral installation is automation—the moment when the behavior no longer feels like effort but simply "how you operate." This isn't magic; it's neuroscience. Automation occurs when a neural pathway becomes strong enough that the brain prioritizes it over older, weaker pathways.

The brain automatizes behaviors for efficiency. It wants to use the least amount of energy possible, so once your new behavior becomes familiar, it becomes the default. This is where identity shifts become permanent and cognitive patterns hold without strain.

Automation is not the beginning of transformation—it is the reward. It is the moment the blueprint becomes reality.

This chapter equips you with every tool needed to move your new behaviors from idea → repetition → consistency → identity → automation.

20 Lessons from Chapter 3

1. New habits require a structural blueprint.
2. Small behaviors are the foundation of new pathways.
3. Consistency cues activate neural readiness.
4. Strategic repetition builds faster wiring.
5. Momentum loops generate dopamine-driven progress.
6. Identity shifts require behavior first.
7. Environment can make or break cognitive installation.
8. Clarity accelerates habit encoding.
9. Emotional anchoring strengthens new behaviors.
10. New behaviors must be tied to meaning to last.
11. Sequencing reduces cognitive overload.
12. Habit stacking speeds installation.
13. Automation occurs when new pathways outcompete old ones.
14. Repetition in similar contexts strengthens wiring.
15. Dopamine rewards accelerate consistency.
16. Tiny habits ignite major transformation.
17. Behavioral design reduces willpower strain.
18. Identity-based habits endure longest.
19. Environmental sculpting removes friction.
20. Your blueprint determines your long-term transformation.

Exercises:

Exercise 1: Create Your Behavior Blueprint

Write down one behavior you want to install.
Define its:

- Cue
- Location
- Time
- Emotion
- Replacement action
- Reward

Exercise 2: Habit Stacking Mini-Plan

Choose one existing habit and attach a new micro-habit to it. Practice for seven days straight.

Exercise 3: Identity Alignment Drill

Write a behavior that your future self performs daily. Practice acting it out once today to begin identity encoding.

10 Journal Prompts

1. What new cognitive behaviors do I want to install this season?
2. Which small version of those behaviors can I start today?
3. What cues can help me activate these behaviors?
4. How can I modify my environment to support them?
5. What emotional anchors will reinforce these behaviors?
6. What identity am I trying to grow into?
7. What momentum loop can I create for early progress?
8. What old habits can I stack new habits onto?
9. What would automation of this new behavior look like in my life?
10. What reward can I give myself for consistency?

Closing Reflection

Installing new cognitive behaviors is the process of telling your brain, "This is who I am becoming." Every cue, every micro-action, every emotionally anchored repetition is a message that shapes your future identity. You are not simply building habits—you are building the architecture of your next evolution. These next 90 days will not just change how you act; they will change who you believe yourself to be. And once the brain accepts the new blueprint, your entire life shifts to reflect it.

Chapter 4: Repetition Protocols – How Consistency Cements Pathways

Why Repetition Is the Oxygen of Change

Repetition is not just something you do—it is the biological force that reshapes your brain's architecture. Without repetition, even the best ideas, habits, or behavioral changes dissolve into noise. With repetition, they become wiring—fast, reliable, resilient pathways that shape your thoughts, actions, and identity.

The brain thrives on patterns. Each repeated behavior sends electrical and chemical signals through the same route over and over again, strengthening the connection. At first, this pathway is fragile. With enough repetition, it becomes the dominant route your brain prefers, even when the behavior is difficult or uncomfortable.

This is why consistency matters more than intensity. A behavior done small, sloppy, imperfectly—but repeated—creates more wiring than a perfect action done once. The brain prioritizes patterns, not performance. Every repetition reinforces your future identity.

Understanding this gives you freedom. You don't need perfection. You need presence. You need participation. And you need repetition—because repetition is what makes change stick.

The Neuroscience of "Wiring In"

When you repeat a behavior, the brain strengthens the synapses involved in that behavior. This strengthening process is called **long-term potentiation (LTP)**. It is the physical mechanism behind learning, memory, and habit formation.

At the beginning of a new behavior, synapses fire weakly and inconsistently. But with repeated activation, the synapses thicken and multiply. They fire faster, more accurately, and with less energy. Eventually, the brain creates a "myelin sheath" around these pathways—an insulating layer that makes the behavior automatic.

This is how you go from "trying to change" to "being changed."

Understanding the biology empowers you to stay consistent during the early phases when the wiring feels unstable. You are not failing. You are in the pre-myelination stage. Keep going, and the brain will catch up.

The best part? Once the pathway is wired, it becomes easier than the old one.

The Repetition Curve: Why It Feels Hard Before It Feels Easy

Every habit has a repetition curve. At first, the brain resists the new pattern because the old pathways still dominate. This resistance stage feels uncomfortable, frustrating, and sometimes confusing. Many people quit here—not because they're incapable, but because they misunderstand the curve.

After enough repetitions, the brain shifts into the adaptation stage. The new pathway begins to form, and the behavior requires less effort. This stage may feel smoother, more predictable, and more emotionally stable.

Beyond adaptation, the curve peaks into automation. This is the moment when the behavior stops requiring conscious effort and becomes part of your identity. The repetition curve is not a straight line—it is a biological progression.

Knowing the curve prevents discouragement. You understand that difficulty is not failure—it is the beginning of wiring.

Frequency Over Duration: Why Short and Often Beats Long and Rare

The brain responds more strongly to frequency than duration. A 2-minute behavior repeated daily builds stronger pathways than a 2-hour behavior done once in a while. This is because neurons require repeated stimulation to form stable connections.

Think of neural wiring like carving lines into soft clay. One deep stroke won't form a reliable groove, but many light strokes will. Frequency creates familiarity. Familiarity reduces neurological resistance. Reduced resistance makes behaviors feel easier, safer, and more natural.

This is why micro-habits are so powerful. They allow you to repeat a behavior without exhaustion. Over time, the brain strengthens the pathway so deeply that the behavior becomes your default.

This is the core of repetition protocol: daily, doable, repeated actions.

Predictable Anchors: Locking New Patterns to Time and Place

Consistency deepens when behaviors occur at predictable times and locations. This is because the brain links the behavior with environmental cues. Over time, these cues trigger the behavior automatically—even before you consciously think about it.

Anchoring behaviors to specific moments (morning, after lunch, before bed) or places (desk, kitchen table, car) removes decision-making friction. The behavior becomes part of the internal rhythm of your day rather than an isolated task you must "remember."

Predictability accelerates encoding because the brain loves patterns. When the same cue triggers the same behavior repeatedly, the pathway cements faster.

Anchors are the structural support beams of repetition. They make consistency easier, which makes rewiring inevitable.

Emotional Repetition: How Feelings Reinforce Pathways

Your brain doesn't just repeat behaviors—it repeats emotional states attached to those behaviors. If a new habit is paired with pride, relief, joy, or confidence, the brain flags the behavior as important and strengthens the pathway faster.

This is why celebrating small wins is not optional—it's neurological reinforcement. Emotional repetition creates emotional familiarity, which signals safety. Once a behavior feels emotionally safe, resistance plummets.

On the other hand, if a habit is constantly paired with stress, resentment, or pressure, the brain may reject it, even if the behavior is beneficial. Emotional overload can short-circuit repetition.

You must attach good feelings to new behaviors. Make them meaningful. Reward yourself. Acknowledge progress. Emotion is the glue of consistency.

Ritualized Repetition: Turning Practice Into Identity

Rituals transform repetition into sacred consistency. A ritual is a predictable sequence that precedes a behavior and signals to the brain that it's time to activate the habit. Rituals reduce chaos, increase focus, and build mental readiness.

For example:

- Lighting a candle before journaling
- Taking a grounding breath before working
- Stretching before exercising
- Clearing your desk before writing

These preparatory actions act as neurological priming. The brain recognizes the ritual and prepares the behavioral pathway for activation. Over time, the ritual becomes just as important as the behavior itself.

Ritualized repetition strengthens identity. It tells your brain:
"This is who I am. This is what I do."

And the brain responds accordingly.

The Dopamine Loop: Rewarding Repetition

Dopamine is the chemical that rewards repeated behavior. When you complete a habit—even a tiny version—dopamine spikes. This spike doesn't just make you feel good; it strengthens the pathway that led to the action.

Dopamine is the biological partner of repetition. Without it, consistency collapses. With it, consistency thrives. This is why small, simple rewards are essential for cognitive installation.

Even checking off a habit box releases dopamine. Acknowledging your consistency—even silently—reinforces wiring. You must intentionally cultivate dopamine within your repetition protocol.

Reward is not indulgence. Reward is neuroplastic strategy.

How the Brain Automates Repetition

Automation is the final phase of neural encoding. It happens when the new pathway becomes more efficient than the old one. Once automated, the behavior requires almost no conscious effort. It becomes who you are, not what you do.

This shift occurs through:

- Myelination
- Predictable cues
- Emotional association
- Identity reinforcement
- Repetition under consistent conditions

Automation is the brain's way of saving energy. It prefers behaviors that are predictable and require minimal cognitive load. Repetition transforms new habits into automatic identity scripts.

Automation is the reward for your commitment. It is the moment the brain takes over and carries the behavior forward effortlessly.

Breaking the "Skip Once" Myth

Many people fear that missing a day ruins their progress—but science reveals the opposite. Missing one repetition does not destroy a neural pathway. Pathways weaken only when absence becomes a pattern.

The "never skip twice" rule is a powerful repetition protocol. If you miss a day, the next day becomes critical. A single repetition reactivates the pathway and prevents significant weakening.

This rule builds resilience. It teaches your brain that consistency is flexible, forgiving, and adaptable—not rigid or punishing.

The pathway thrives on pattern, not perfection.

Stacking Repetitions for Maximum Impact

Repetition becomes stronger when you layer habits in sequences. For example:

- Breath → Write → Plan
- Water → Stretch → Work
- Candle → Journal → Reflect

Stacking creates a chain reaction. One behavior activates the next. This multiplies the effect of repetition because each habit reinforces the others through associative wiring.

Habit stacking turns a single repetition into a cluster of repetitions. This accelerates encoding and makes the entire sequence easier to maintain.

Stacks are the power tools of the repetition protocol. They create waterfalls of consistency.

Consistency as a Self-Identity Practice

Ultimately, repetition isn't just a behavior—it's an identity statement. Every repeated action tells your brain:
"This is who I am now."

The more often you repeat a behavior, the faster your identity shifts. Identity-based behaviors become self-sustaining because the brain protects the habits that define you.

When consistency becomes part of your identity, you no longer force yourself to act—you follow your wiring. This is the deepest level of transformation. This is how you become your future self.

Repetition is identity in motion.

20 Lessons from Chapter 4

1. Repetition is the foundation of neural change.
2. LTP physically strengthens pathways.
3. Wiring feels hard before it feels easy.
4. Frequency builds habits faster than duration.
5. Behavioral anchors enhance consistency.
6. Emotional reinforcement accelerates encoding.
7. Rituals prepare the brain for action.
8. Dopamine rewards repeated behavior.
9. Automation occurs when new pathways outperform old ones.
10. Missing once does not destroy progress.
11. "Never skip twice" protects the pathway.
12. Habit stacking multiplies repetition.
13. Consistency forms identity.
14. Predictable cues accelerate wiring.
15. Small wins train dopamine loops.
16. The brain prioritizes repeated patterns over intense ones.
17. Emotional safety enhances consistency.
18. Repetition thrives on clarity and simplicity.
19. Rituals create neural priming.
20. Repetition is the bridge from effort to identity.

Exercises:

Exercise 1: Set Your Daily Repetition Protocol

Choose one behavior and define how you will repeat it daily for 2 minutes.
Keep it small. Keep it consistent.

Exercise 2: Create a Ritual Cue

Design one 15–30 second ritual that precedes your new behavior.
Repeat this ritual every day.

Exercise 3: "Never Skip Twice" Tracker

Create a simple checklist for 14 days.

Mark each day with:
✓ Repeated
X Missed
Circle the next day after a miss to enforce the rule.

10 Journal Prompts

1. What behavior do I need to repeat every day to become my next-level self?
2. What cues can I attach to this repetition?
3. What ritual can I use to prepare my brain?
4. What emotional reward can I attach?
5. What makes repetition difficult for me?
6. Where can I reduce friction?
7. When in my day am I most consistent?
8. What does automation of this habit look like in my life?
9. What identity does this habit support?
10. What "never skip twice" rule do I want to adopt?

Closing Reflection

Repetition is the silent architect of transformation. Every time you show up—even for two minutes—you carve new wiring into your brain. You teach yourself that change is possible, sustainable, and natural. These repeated moments create the foundation of your future identity. You are not practicing a habit—you are practicing who you are becoming. With every repetition, you cement the life you want into the neural pathways that will carry you there.

Chapter 5: Integration Season – Maintaining Your Rewired Mind

Integration: Where Transformation Becomes a Lifestyle

Integration is the phase where all your rewiring—your new habits, cognitive shifts, and identity frameworks—merge into your daily life. It's the season where your mind stops "learning" the new pattern and begins **living** it. Just like a garden that's been nurtured through winter sprouting toward spring, your rewired mind is ready to express its new growth.

Integration is not about adding more. It's about maintaining what you've already built. Once the pathways are established, your job is to preserve them with steady reinforcement. This is where change becomes self-sustaining. Instead of pushing your mind, you guide it gently into consistency, allowing your rewired circuits to strengthen without strain.

This season requires patience. You are shifting from transformation mode to stabilization mode, and the brain thrives on stability. The more predictable your new behaviors become, the deeper the wiring embeds. Integration is not dramatic—it's deliberate.

The goal of this chapter is to help you maintain your new wiring so it becomes part of your everyday identity—not a temporary upgrade, but a permanent evolution.

Stability Over Intensity: Why Maintenance Creates Mastery

When your brain is freshly rewired, it is strong but still young. These circuits need stability to mature. Many people relapse into old patterns because they switch too quickly from consistency to intensity. They attempt to expand, accelerate, or overcommit before the wiring is ready.

Maintenance may feel slower, quieter, or less exciting—but this phase is where mastery truly forms. Stability allows the brain to settle into its new configuration. It smooths rough edges, reduces cognitive resistance, and transforms effort-based actions into natural rhythms.

This is also the phase where emotional stability becomes crucial. When your emotions are regulated, your wiring embeds more cleanly. When your emotions spike too often, the brain becomes reactive and may revert to old pathways.

In integration, your job is not to dramatically push but to deeply anchor. You are teaching your mind that this new version of you is safe, reliable, and sustainable.

The "Identity Set Point": Protecting Your New Neural Default

Every person has a subconscious identity set point: the level of behavior, emotion, and habit their brain considers "normal." Your rewiring journey has elevated your identity, and during integration, you teach your brain that this new level is your new normal.

This is one of the most crucial aspects of maintaining your rewired mind. Old patterns may briefly try to resurface because they represent past set points. But if you continue reinforcing the new identity, the brain updates its internal baseline.

Identity set points change through consistent action paired with emotional affirmation. When you repeatedly behave like your future self, and feel good about it, the brain shifts its expectations.

Integration season is where you lock in that shift. You move from "I am becoming" to "I am." The set point adjusts. Your identity stabilizes. Your wiring becomes permanent.

The Return of Old Patterns: Why They Resurface and How to Respond

Even after strong rewiring, old patterns may briefly reappear. This is not regression; it is the brain testing whether those pathways are still valid. Think of it as a system scan—an internal check to confirm which circuits should remain active.

During integration, your response to these resurgences determines the outcome. If you panic or shame yourself, the old pathway gains emotional reinforcement. If you respond with neutrality and pattern interruption, the old pathway weakens further.

When an old pattern appears, say to yourself:

"This is a memory of who I used to be, not who I am."

This separates past identity from current wiring. Your ability to handle these moments with calm clarity is what prevents relapse and deepens transformation.

Old patterns lose their power when you stop feeding them attention.

Maintenance Rituals: Protecting Your Cognitive Garden

Every rewired mind requires maintenance rituals—small, consistent practices that reinforce your new pathways. These rituals keep your mind aligned with your identity and prevent subtle slippage that can happen during busy, stressful, or uncertain times.

Maintenance rituals do not need to be long or complicated. They simply need to be consistent. Examples include:

- A morning intention statement
- A nightly reflection ritual
- A weekly reset session
- A grounding breath before major tasks
- A 3-minute identity reinforcement practice

These rituals act like watering and tending your cognitive garden. Without them, weeds may return quietly. With them, your mental environment stays clear and healthy.

Integration season is not about doing more—it's about doing what matters consistently.

Cognitive Flexibility: Staying Adaptable While Staying Aligned

Maintaining a rewired mind does not mean becoming rigid. True cognitive health requires flexibility—the ability to adapt while still remaining anchored. Flexibility allows your brain to handle unexpected changes without dissolving your wiring.

Cognitive flexibility is built through subtle shifts: taking a new route, learning something unfamiliar, responding differently to stress, experimenting with timing, or adjusting your environment. These small exposures prevent stagnation and strengthen overall neural resilience.

In integration, flexibility works alongside stability. Stability anchors your identity; flexibility keeps it alive, dynamic, and relevant. Together, they form a powerful mental ecosystem.

The goal is a mind that is rooted, but not stuck. Open, but not chaotic. Rewired, but still evolving.

Emotional Regulation as a Rewiring Shield

Your emotional state is a direct influence on your neural maintenance. Emotions that spike frequently—fear, overwhelm, anger, shame—can disrupt your new pathways because they activate the survival circuits that belonged to your old identity.

This makes emotional regulation a shield for your rewiring. Practices such as deep breathing, grounding exercises, brief pauses, or journaling help you stay regulated. When emotions rise, your prefrontal cortex remains active, allowing your new wiring to stay in control.

Regulation does not mean suppressing emotions. It means responding consciously rather than reactively. It means creating space between the feeling and the behavior.

A regulated nervous system preserves your rewiring—and supports long-term identity stability.

Strengthening the New Neural Dominion

Your new identity is a territory reclaimed from old patterns. Integration season is where you strengthen that dominion. Every time you choose the new pathway over the old one, you fortify the new route and weaken the old route further.

This strengthening rarely requires major actions. It often happens in small, subtle ways: responding with calm instead of panic, choosing clarity instead of avoidance, following through instead of hesitating.

Your brain learns dominance through repetition and emotional reinforcement. When the new pathway consistently wins the internal election, it becomes the ruling circuit.

This is how identities become unshakeable—not through intensity, but through long-term neural dominance.

The Seasonal Mindset: Why Your Brain Needs Cycles

Just like the natural world, the brain works in cycles. Integration season acknowledges this biological truth. You are not meant to push endlessly; you are meant to grow, stabilize, integrate, and then grow again.

Cycles prevent burnout. They allow the brain to rest between periods of change. They provide space for reflection and assimilation. Integration season aligns with the natural rhythm of winter—quiet, reflective, consolidating, preparing for spring.

When you honor this rhythm, your rewiring becomes sustainable. You learn to work with your biology instead of against it. You learn that renewal is strongest after seasons of rest and consolidation.

This chapter symbolizes your winter of the mind—the preparation for the bloom ahead.

Rewiring Relationships: Protecting Your Growth Environment

Your mind does not exist in isolation. Your relationships, environment, and daily interactions influence your wiring. During integration season, you must evaluate what supports your new pathways and what undermines them.

Some relationships reinforce your identity growth. Others reinforce your past. Some environments encourage clarity and focus. Others trigger old emotional loops. Integration is the time to set boundaries, adjust your surroundings, or redefine how you engage with certain individuals.

Protecting your rewiring is not selfish—it is necessary. You cannot maintain a new identity in a space designed for your old one.

Your growth environment becomes part of your long-term neural health.

Long-Term Reinforcement: Building a Future-Proof Identity

Maintaining a rewired mind requires long-term reinforcement. Even deeply embedded neural pathways strengthen with use. This means your identity transformation is built through years of aligned actions—not just months.

However, reinforcement does not require rigidity or perfection. It simply requires consistency in the direction of your future self. When you continue practicing identity-based behaviors—no matter how small—you reinforce the architecture of your mind.

Long-term reinforcement ensures that your transformation survives stress, transitions, and time. It protects your wiring from erosion and keeps your identity evolving toward your highest potential.

Your rewired mind is not fragile—it is adaptive. With reinforcement, it becomes unstoppable.

The Integrated Self: Becoming Who You Were Training For

Integration season culminates in a profound shift: you stop practicing the identity and start *being* it. This is the moment your brain stops treating your new habits as "new" and begins treating them as your normal operating system.

The integrated self is calm, grounded, consistent, and aligned. Your behaviors reflect your identity, and your identity supports your behaviors. The loop becomes harmonious. You no longer battle your mind; you work with it.

This stage is not a finish line—it is a foundation. A starting point for deeper growth, bigger dreams, and more satisfying experiences. Integration is the moment you meet the version of you that your rewiring has prepared.

This is the self you were building toward all along.

20 Lessons from Chapter 5

1. Integration stabilizes new neural pathways.
2. Stability anchors identity.
3. Old patterns may resurface as memory, not regression.
4. Maintenance rituals protect your mental ecosystem.
5. Emotional regulation shields new wiring.
6. Flexibility keeps rewiring dynamic and resilient.
7. Identity set points must be updated through consistency.
8. Environment influences long-term maintenance.
9. Reinforcement keeps the pathways strong.
10. Repetition during this phase cements identity.
11. Old pathways weaken through lack of emotional fuel.
12. Patterns test themselves before dissolving.
13. Integration is quiet but powerful work.
14. Boundaries support cognitive stability.
15. Long-term identity requires ongoing alignment.
16. Rituals reduce erosion of new habits.
17. Emotional neutrality weakens old loops.
18. Maintenance is mastery in disguise.
19. Integration prepares the mind for future evolution.
20. You become the integrated self through lived repetition.

Exercises:

Exercise 1: Identity Set Point Reset

Write your future identity in one sentence.
Repeat it daily during integration season to establish your baseline.

Exercise 2: Maintenance Ritual Builder

Choose one behavior to maintain.
Build a 30–60 second ritual that supports it and perform it for 14 days.

Exercise 3: Pattern Memory Neutralizer

When an old pattern appears, write a 1–2 sentence neutral response like:
"This is my past, not my present."
Repeat each time the loop resurfaces to weaken emotional attachment.

10 Journal Prompts

1. What parts of my rewired identity feel the strongest?
2. What areas need more maintenance?
3. Which old patterns attempt to return, and how do I respond?
4. What rituals keep me grounded and aligned?
5. What relationships support my transformation?
6. What environments anchor my new behavior?
7. What boundaries protect my identity?
8. How does my integrated self think and act daily?
9. What emotional states help reinforce my new wiring?
10. What does maintaining this identity look like long-term?

Closing Reflection

Integration season is the moment your transformation becomes truth. You have rewired your pathways, your identity, and your internal operating system. Now you step into stability—not as someone trying to change, but as someone who *has* changed. This season is where your growth becomes real, where your new identity becomes home, and where your rewired mind begins shaping the life you were always capable of living. You are not returning to who you were—you are expanding into who you've become. And this integrated self will lead you into every spring that follows.

Appendix A: 100 Journal Prompts for Your 90-Day Rewire

1. What thought patterns am I most ready to release?
2. Which old identity no longer fits who I am becoming?
3. What habits drain my energy the most?
4. What habits give me the most energy?
5. What does my "rewired self" feel like on a normal day?
6. What does my future self no longer tolerate?
7. What triggers activate my old patterns?
8. What physical sensations signal the start of a loop?
9. What emotions tend to pull me backward?
10. What emotions tend to move me forward?
11. What loop did I interrupt today?
12. What loop am I avoiding interrupting?
13. What fear lies underneath my sabotaging habits?
14. What belief is blocking my progress?
15. What belief am I ready to install?
16. What behavior would my next-level identity choose right now?
17. What environment supports the person I'm becoming?
18. What environment weakens the person I'm becoming?
19. Who do I want to be when spring arrives?
20. How do I want to feel 90 days from now?
21. What inner narrative needs rewriting?
22. What do I repeat that keeps me small?
23. What do I repeat that grows me?
24. What emotion do I want to experience more often?
25. What emotion am I ready to experience less often?
26. What behaviors reassure my nervous system?
27. What behaviors agitate my nervous system?
28. What needs to be simplified in my life?
29. What needs to be made more intentional?
30. What small habit could change everything if repeated daily?

31. How does my body respond to change?
32. How does my mind respond to stability?
33. What do I procrastinate on and why?
34. What identity am I afraid of stepping into?
35. What identity am I excited to step into?
36. What pattern from my childhood still influences me?
37. What pattern from my past self must end now?
38. What gives me momentum?
39. What steals my momentum?
40. What makes me feel emotionally grounded?
41. What makes me feel emotionally spiraled?
42. What does "rewiring" mean to me personally?
43. What story about myself am I ready to release?
44. What story about myself am I ready to begin?
45. What would I do if fear wasn't present?
46. What inner voice do I want to amplify?
47. What inner voice do I want to silence?
48. What does a mentally clear day look like for me?
49. What does a mentally cluttered day feel like?
50. Which habits feel misaligned with my future identity?
51. Which habits support my transformation?
52. When do I feel most like myself?
53. When do I feel disconnected from myself?
54. What did I learn about my patterns this week?
55. What did I learn about my resilience this week?
56. What would my life look like with consistent habits?
57. What would my life look like if old loops dissolved?
58. What small win am I most proud of today?
59. What resistance did I overcome today?
60. What resistance is still strong?
61. What helps me return to clarity?
62. What clouds my thinking?
63. What boundary would support my rewiring?

64. What boundary am I afraid to set?
65. What do I want to consciously repeat more often?
66. What do I want to consciously repeat less?
67. What is one identity-based action I can repeat daily?
68. What am I becoming more aware of lately?
69. Where am I growing fastest?
70. Where am I growing slowest?
71. What habit feels easiest to maintain and why?
72. What habit feels hardest and why?
73. What motivates me to improve myself?
74. What discourages me the most?
75. What makes me feel mentally strong?
76. What makes me feel mentally tired?
77. How do I know when I'm aligned with my future self?
78. What does misalignment feel like in my body?
79. What emotional cycles repeat most often?
80. What emotional cycles am I breaking?
81. What thought pattern is loosening its grip on me?
82. What thought pattern still has power over me?
83. What reinforces my new identity?
84. What tempts me back into my old identity?
85. What do I need to hear more often?
86. What do I need to stop telling myself?
87. What daily ritual helps me reset?
88. What daily ritual no longer serves me?
89. What does "progress" look like without perfection?
90. What does "consistency" look like in my real life?
91. What would make rewiring feel easier?
92. What would make rewiring feel meaningful?
93. What am I letting go of this month?
94. What am I building this month?
95. What am I reclaiming this month?
96. What kind of inner peace do I want to cultivate?

97. What kind of inner power do I want to activate?
98. What will I remember most about this 90-day journey?
99. What kind of person will I be by spring?
100. What identity am I choosing—intentionally—today?

Closing Reflection

You have spent these pages witnessing your mind with honesty, shaping your identity with intention, and cultivating clarity through every question you answered. These 100 journal prompts were not just exercises—they were neural invitations. Every reflection softened an old loop. Every insight strengthened a new one. Every moment of awareness moved you closer to the version of yourself who will rise fully when spring arrives.

Rewiring is never a single breakthrough. It is a quiet accumulation of choices—attention shifted, habits interrupted, emotions understood, identity rewritten one small decision at a time. Through this practice, you have proven that your mind is not fixed. It is responsive, alive, and willing to grow when given direction.

As you close this appendix, remember that you are not returning to who you were before you began. You are walking forward as someone who can see their own patterns, name their own triggers, choose their own behaviors, and shape their own future. You are building a mind that supports your purpose instead of sabotaging it. A mind that opens instead of collapses. A mind preparing to bloom.

Your 90-day transformation is not just possible—it has already begun.

Message from the Author:

I hope you enjoyed this book, I love astrology and knew there was not a book such as this out on the shelf. I love metaphysical items as well. Please check out my other books:

-Life of Government Benefits

-My life of Hell

-My life with Hydrocephalus

-Red Sky

-World Domination:Woman's rule

-World Domination:Woman's Rule 2: The War

-Life and Banishment of Apophis: book 1

-The Kidney Friendly Diet

-The Ultimate Hemp Cookbook

-Creating a Dispensary(legally)

-Cleanliness throughout life: the importance of showering from childhood to adulthood.

-Strong Roots: The Risks of Overcoddling children

-Hemp Horoscopes: Cosmic Insights and Earthly Healing

- Celestial Hemp Navigating the Zodiac: Through the Green Cosmos

-Astrological Hemp: Aligning The Stars with Earth's Ancient Herb

-The Astrological Guide to Hemp: Stars, Signs, and Sacred Leaves

-Green Growth: Innovative Marketing Strategies for your Hemp Products and Dispensary

-Cosmic Cannabis

-Astrological Munchies

-Henry The Hemp

-Zodiacal Roots: The Astrological Soul Of Hemp

- **Green Constellations: Intersection of Hemp and Zodiac**

-Hemp in The Houses: An astrological Adventure Through The Cannabis Galaxy

-Galactic Ganja Guide
Heavenly Hemp
Zodiac Leaves
Doctor Who Astrology
Cannastrology
Stellar Satvias and Cosmic Indicas
Celestial Cannabis: A Zodiac Journey
AstroHerbology: The Sky and The Soil: Volume 1
AstroHerbology:Celestial Cannabis:Volume 2
Cosmic Cannabis Cultivation
The Starry Guide to Herbal Harmony: Volume 1
The Starry Guide to Herbal Harmony: Cannabis Universe: Volume 2
Yugioh Astrology: Astrological Guide to Deck, Duels and more
Nightmare Mansion: Echoes of The Abyss
Nightmare Mansion 2: Legacy of Shadows
Nightmare Mansion 3: Shadows of the Forgotten
Nightmare Mansion 4: Echoes of the Damned
The Life and Banishment of Apophis: Book 2
Nightmare Mansion: Halls of Despair
Healing with Herb: Cannabis and Hydrocephalus
Planetary Pot: Aligning with Astrological Herbs: Volume 1
Fast Track to Freedom: 30 Days to Financial Independence Using AI, Assets, and Agile Hustles
Cosmic Hemp Pathways
How to Become Financially Free in 30 Days: 10,000 Paths to Prosperity
Zodiacal Herbage: Astrological Insights: Volume 1
Nightmare Mansion: Whispers in the Walls
The Daleks Invade Atlantis
Henry the hemp and Hydrocephalus

10X The Kidney Friendly Diet

Cannabis Universe: Adult coloring book

Hemp Astrology: The Healing Power of the Stars

Zodiacal Herbage: Astrological Insights: Cannabis Universe: Volume 2

Planetary Pot: Aligning with Astrological Herbs: Cannabis Universes: Volume 2

Doctor Who: Convergence Protocol – The Replicator War

Nightmare Mansion: Curse of the Blood Moon

The Celestial Stoner: A Guide to the Zodiac

Cosmic Pleasures: Sex Toy Astrology for Every Sign

Hydrocephalus Astrology: Navigating the Stars and Healing Waters

Lapis and the Mischievous Chocolate Bar

Celestial Positions: Sexual Astrology for Every Sign

Apophis's Shadow Work Journal: : A Journey of Self-Discovery and Healing

Kinky Cosmos: Sexual Kink Astrology for Every Sign

Digital Cosmos: The Astrological Digimon Compendium

Stellar Seeds: The Cosmic Guide to Growing with Astrology

Apophis's Daily Gratitude Journal

Cat Astrology: Feline Mysteries of the Cosmos

The Cosmic Kama Sutra: An Astrological Guide to Sexual Positions

Unleash Your Potential: A Guided Journal Powered by AI Insights

Whispers of the Enchanted Grove

Cosmic Pleasures: An Astrological Guide to Sexual Kinks

369, 12 Manifestation Journal

Whisper of the nocturne journal(blank journal for writing or drawing)

The Boogey Book

Locked In Reflection: A Chastity Journey Through Locktober

Generating Wealth Quickly:How to Generate $100,000 in 24 Hours

Star Magic: Harness the Power of the Universe

The Flatulence Chronicles: A Fart Journal for Self-Discovery

The Doctor and The Death Moth

Seize the Day: A Personal Seizure Tracking Journal

The Ultimate Boogeyman Safari: A Journey into the Boogie World and Beyond

Whispers of Samhain: 1,000 Spells of Love, Luck, and Lunar Magic: Samhain Spell Book

Apophis's guides:Witch's Spellbook Crafting Guide for Halloween

Frost & Flame: The Enchanted Yule Grimoire of 1000 Winter Spells

The Ultimate Boogey Goo Guide & Spooky Activities for Halloween Fun

Harmony of the Scales: A Libra's Spellcraft for Balance and Beauty

The Enchanted Advent: 36 Days of Christmas Wonders

Nightmare Mansion: The Labyrinth of Screams

Harvest of Enchantment: 1,000 Spells of Gratitude, Love, and Fortune for Thanksgiving

The Boogey Chronicles: A Journal of Nightly Encounters and Shadowy Secrets

The 12 Days of Financial Freedom: A Step-by-Step Christmas Countdown to Transform Your Finances

Sigil of the Eternal Spiral Blank Journal

A Christmas Feast: Timeless Recipes for Every Meal

Holiday Stress-Free Solutions: A Survival Guide to Thriving During the Festive Season

Yu-Gi-Oh! Holiday Gifting Mastery: The Ultimate Guide for Fans and Newcomers Alike

Holiday Harmony: A Hydrocephalus Survival Guide for the Festive Season

Celestial Craft: The Witch's Almanac for 2025 – A Cosmic Guide to Manifestations, Moons, and Mystical Events

Doctor Who: The Toymaker's Winter Wonderland

Tulsa King Unveiled: A Thrilling Guide to Stallone's Mafia Masterpiece

Pendulum Craft: A Complete Guide to Crafting and Using Personalized Divination Tools

Nightmare Mansion: Santa's Eternal Eve

Starlight Noel: A Cosmic Journey through Christmas Mysteries

The Dark Architect: Unlocking the Blueprint of Existence

Surviving the Embrace: The Ultimate Guide to Encounters with The Hugging Molly

The Enchanted Codex: Secrets of the Craft for Witches, Wiccans, and Pagans

Harvest of Gratitude: A Complete Thanksgiving Guide

Yuletide Essentials: A Complete Guide to an Authentic and Magical Christmas

Celestial Smokes: A Cosmic Guide to Cigars and Astrology

Living in Balance: A Comprehensive Survival Guide to Thriving with Diabetes Insipidus

Cosmic Symbiosis: The Venom Zodiac Chronicles

The Cursed Paw of Ambition

Cosmic Symbiosis: The Astrological Venom Journal

Celestial Wonders Unfold: A Stargazer's Guide to the Cosmos (2024-2029)

The Ultimate Black Friday Prepper's Guide: Mastering Shopping Strategies and Savings

Cosmic Sales: The Astrological Guide to Black Friday Shopping

Legends of the Corn Mother and Other Harvest Myths

Whispers of the Harvest: The Corn Mother's Journal
The Evergreen Spellbook
The Doctor Meets the Boogeyman
The White Witch of Rose Hall's SpellBook
The Gingerbread Golem's Shadow: A Study in Sweet Darkness
The Gingerbread Golem Codex: An Academic Exploration of Sweet Myths
The Gingerbread Golem Grimoire: Sweet Magicks and Spells for the Festive Witch
The Curse of the Gingerbread Golem
10-minute Christmas Crafts for kids
Christmas Crisis Solutions: The Ultimate Last-Minute Survival Guide
Gingerbread Golem Recipes: Holiday Treats with a Magical Twist
The Infinite Key: Unlocking Mystical Secrets of the Ages
Enchanted Yule: A Wiccan and Pagan Guide to a Magical and Memorable Season
Dinosaurs of Power: Unlocking Ancient Magick
Astro-Dinos: The Cosmic Guide to Prehistoric Wisdom
Gallifrey's Yule Logs: A Festive Doctor Who Cookbook
The Dino Grimoire: Secrets of Prehistoric Magick
The Gift They Never Knew They Needed
The Gingerbread Golem's Culinary Alchemy: Enchanting Recipes for a Sweetly Dark Feast
A Time Lord Christmas: Holiday Adventures with the Doctor
Krampusproofing Your Home: Defensive Strategies for Yule
Silent Frights: A Collection of Christmas Creepypastas to Chill Your Bones
Santa Raptor's Jolly Carnage: A Dino-Claus Christmas Tale
Prehistoric Palettes: A Dino Wicca Coloring Journey
The Christmas Wishkeeper Chronicles
The Starlight Sleigh: A Holiday Journey
Elf Secrets: The True Magic of the North Pole

Candy Cane Conjurations

Cooking with Kids: Recipes Under 20 Minutes

Doctor Who: The TARDIS Confiscation

The Anxiety First Aid Kit: Quick Tools to Calm Your Mind

Frosty Whispers: A Winter's Tale

The Infinite Key: Unlocking the Secrets to Prosperity, Resilience, and Purpose

The Grasping Void: Why You'll Regret This Purchase

Astrology for Busy Bees: Star Signs Simplified

The Instant Focus Formula: Cut Through the Noise

The Secret Language of Colors: Unlocking the Emotional Codes

Sacred Fossil Chronicles: Blank Journal

The Christmas Cottage Miracle

Feeding Frenzy: Graboid-Inspired Recipes

Manifest in Minutes: The Quick Law of Attraction Guide

The Symbiote Chronicles: Doctor Who's Venomous Journey

Think Tiny, Grow Big: The Minimalist Mindset

The Energy Key: Unlocking Limitless Motivation

New Year, New Magic: Manifesting Your Best Year Yet

Unstoppable You: Mastering Confidence in Minutes

Infinite Energy: The Secret to Never Feeling Drained

Lightning Focus: Mastering the Art of Productivity in a Distracted World

Saturnalia Manifestation Magick: A Guide to Unlocking Abundance During the Solstice

Graboids and Garland: The Ultimate Tremors-Themed Christmas Guide

12 Nights of Holiday Magic

The Power of Pause: 60-Second Mindfulness Practices

The Quick Reset: How to Reclaim Your Life After Burnout

The Shadow Eater: A Tale of Despair and Survival

The Micro-Mastery Method: Transform Your Skills in Just Minutes a Day

Reclaiming Time: How to Live More by Doing Less
Chronovore: The Eternal Nexus
The Mind Reset: Unlocking Your Inner Peace in a Chaotic World
Confidence Code: Building Unshakable Self-Belief
Baby the Vampire Terrier
Baby the Vampire Terrier's Christmas Adventure
Celestial Streams: The Content Creator's Astrology Manual
The Wealth Whisperer: Unlocking Abundance with Everyday Actions
The Energy Equation: Maximize Your Output Without Burning Out
The Happiness Algorithm: Science-Backed Steps to Joyful Living
Stress-Free Success: Achieving Goals Without Anxiety
Mindful Wealth: The New Blueprint for Financial Freedom
The Festive Flavors of New Year: A Culinary Celebration
The Master's Gambit: Keys of Eternal Power
Shadowed Secrets: Groundhog Day Mysteries
Beneath the Burrow: Lessons from the Groundhog
Spring's Whispers: The Groundhog's Prediction
The Limitless Mindset: Unlock Your Untapped Potential
The Focus Funnel: How to Cut Through Chaos and Get Results
Bold Moves: Building Courage to Live on Your Terms
The Daily Shift: Simple Practices for Lasting Transformation
The Quarter-Life Reset: Thriving in Your 20s and 30s
The Art of Shadowplay: Building Your Own Personal Myth
The Eternal Loop: Finding Purpose in Repetition
Burrowing Wisdom: Life Lessons from the Groundhog
Shadow Work: A Groundhog Day Perspective
Love in Bloom: 5-Minute Romantic Gestures
The Shadowspell Codex: Secrets of Forbidden Magick
The Burnout Cure: Finding Balance in a Busy World
The Groundhog Prophecy: Unlocking Seasonal Secrets
Nog Tales: The Spirited History of Eggnog

Six More Weeks: Embracing Seasonal Transitions
The Lumivian Chronicles: Fragments of the Fifth Dimension
Money on Your Mind: A Beginner's Guide to Wealth
The Focus Fix: Breaking Through Distraction
January's Spirit Keepers: Mystical Protectors of the Cold
Creativity Unchained: Unlocking Your Wildest Ideas in 2025
Manifestation Mastery: 365 Days to Rewrite Your Reality
The Groundhog's Mirror: Reflecting on Change
The Weeping Angels' Christmas Curse
Burrowed in Time: A Groundhog Day Journey
Heartbeats: Poems to Share with Your Valentine
Dino Wicca: The Sacred Grimoire of Prehistoric Magick
Courage of the Pride: Finding Your Inner Roar
The Lion's Leap: Bold Moves for Big Results
Healthy Hustle: Achieving Without Overworking
Practical Manifesting: Turning Dreams into Reality in 2025
Jurassic Pharaohs: Unlocking the Magick of Ancient Egypt and Dino Wicca
The Happiness Equation: Small Changes for Big Joy
The Confidence Compass: Finding Your Inner Strength
Whispers in the Hollow: Tales of the Forgotten Beasts
Echoes from the Hollow: The Return of Forgotten Beasts
The Hollow Ascendant: The Rise of the Forgotten Beasts
The Relationship Reset: Building Better Connections
Mastering the Morning: How to Win the Day Before 8 AM
The Shadow's Dance: Groundhog Day Symbolism
Cupid's Kitchen: Quick Valentine's Day Recipes
Valentine's Day on a Budget: Love Without Breaking the Bank
Astrocraft: Aligning the Stars in the World of Minecraft
Forecasting Life: Groundhog Day Reflections
Bleeding Hearts: Twisted Tales of Valentine's Terror
Herbal Smoke Revolution: The Ultimate Guide to Nature's Cigarette Alternative

Winter's Wrath: The Complete Survival Blueprint for Extreme Freezes.

The Groundhog's Shadow: A Tale of Seasons

Burrowed Insights: Wisdom from the Groundhog

Sensual Strings: The Art of Erotic Bondage

Whispered Flames: Unlocking the Power of Fire Play

Forgotten Shadows: A Guide to Cryptids Lost to Time

Six Weeks of Secrets: Groundhog Day's Hidden Messages

Shadows and Cycles: Groundhog Day Reflections

The Art of Love Letters: Crafting the Perfect Message

Romantic Getaways at Home: Turning Your Space into Paradise

Purrfect Brews: A Cat Lover's Guide to Coffee and Companionship

The Groundhog's Wisdom: Timeless Lessons for Modern Life

The Shadow Oracle: Groundhog Day as a Predictor

Emerging from the Burrow: A Journey of Renewal

The Language of Love: Learning Your Partner's Love Style

Authorpreneur: The Ultimate Blueprint for Writing, Publishing, and Thriving as an Author

Weathering the Seasons: Groundhog Day Perspectives

Valentine's Day Magic: A Guide to Romantic Rituals

The Shadow Chronicles: Stories of Groundhog Day

Love and Laughter: Fun Games for Valentine's Day

AstroRealty: Unlocking the Stars for Property Success

The Groundhog's Path: A Guide to Seasonal Balance

Groundhog Day Diaries: Reflections in the Shadow

The Groundhog's Light: Illuminating the Path Ahead

Valentine's Traditions from Around the World

AI Wealth Revolution: Unlocking the Trillionaire Mindset

Love Rekindled: Reigniting Passion in Relationships

Single and Thriving: Self-Love on Valentine's Day

Emerald Legends: Mystical Tales of Ireland

Green Alchemy: Harnessing Nature's Magic
The Hearts of Horror: A Valentine's Day Nightmare
The Leprechaun's Guide to Wealth and Wisdom
Dancing with the Sidhe: Celebrating the Otherworld
Shamrocks and Shadows: Mysteries of the Green Isle
Emerald Energy: Harnessing Luck and Growth
The Gingerbread Golem's Valentine: A Sweetheart's Guide to Love and Enchantment
The Celtic Knot: Weaving Life and Destiny
Green Fire: Elemental Magic for St. Patrick's Day
Clover Chronicles: Finding Your Inner Luck
Ireland's Mystical Creatures: A Field Guide
Gingerbread Golem's Love Almanac
Prowl and Thrive: The Lion's Guide to Success
Love Alchemy: Transforming Your Life Through Heart Energy
WORLD DOMINATION: Woman's Rule 3:The New Life
The Midnight Rose: A Guide to Lunar Love Spells
The Forbidden Letters: Writing Your Own Love Prophecy
Luck and Lore: St. Patrick's Day for Modern Mystics
The Green Path: A Pagan Celebration of Renewal
The Dark Architect's Guide to Reprogramming Reality
Prankster's Paradise: A Guide to Harmless Hijinks
Manifest Your Reality: The Law of Attraction Simplified
The TARDIS Owner's Manual: Understanding the Doctor's Ship: *A complete guide to the TARDIS, its technology, secrets, and mysteries*
Starlit Romance: Astrology Secrets for Finding True Love
The Time Lord's Atlas: A Complete Guide to the Whoniverse: *A breakdown of the locations, planets, and dimensions explored in Doctor Who*
Sweetheart Shadows: The Dark Side of Love and Attraction
February Fire: Reigniting Passion in Every Area of Life

The Self-Love Toolkit: 5 Ways to Embrace Who You Are

February Sparks: Ignite Your Dreams in 28 Days

March to Success: A 31-Day Action Blueprint

Ancient Paths: The 13 Sacred Principles of Dino Wicca

Echoes of Tomorrow: Navigating the AI Revolution

The Wellness Blueprint: Balancing Mind, Body, and Soul

Green Horizons: Sustainable Living for a Better Tomorrow

The AI Wealth Code: How to Make Millions with Automation

AI-Powered Creativity: Writing, Art, and Music for Profit

Extinction Rites: Rebirthing Your Soul Through Prehistoric Magick

Sacred Serpents tarot

Celestial Enchantment blank journal

Star Strains

Culinary Journeys: Exploring Global Flavors at Home

The Hollowvale Curse

The Hollowvale Harvest

The Egg of Transformation: Awakening Your Inner Power

Blooming Into Power: A Wiccan Guide to Spring Awakening

The Nightmare Nexus: The Third Doctor's Perilous Haunting

Digital Detox: Reclaiming Your Life in a Connected World

Ostara's Path: Walking the Spiral of Renewal

The Sacred Hare

Financial Freedom: Building Wealth in the Modern Age

Spring's Cauldron: Stirring the Waters of Change

The Hollowvale Pact

Quantum Consciousness: The Science of Reality Shifting

The Hollowvale Hunger

The Sacred Waters Within: A Witch's Guide to Hydrocephalus Magick

The Raven's Nest: Building a Life of Unshakable Stability

AI and the Human Mind: The Future of Intelligence

The Hollowvale Reckoning

Timeless Love: Building and Maintaining Lasting Relationships

The Raven's Roar: Unlocking Unstoppable Confidence

Raven Sight: Awakening Intuition and Inner Wisdom

The Butterfly Effect: Small Changes, Big Transformations

Taming the Boogeyman: How to Conquer Your Inner Fears

The Magick of Green: Awakening Earth's Energy in You

The Entrepreneurial Mindset: Secrets to Business Success

The Hollowvale End

The Shadow Luck Ritual: Reclaiming Power from Your Dark Side

Spring Magick for Beginners: A Simple Guide to Seasonal Energy Work

Doctor Who: The Hollowvale Conundrum

The March of Miracles: Unlocking Synchronicities in Spring

Unveiling the Cosmos: A Guide to Stargazing and Space Exploration

The Ultimate Guide to Surviving an Economic Collapse

The AI Gold Rush: How to Profit from the AI Revolution

Bastet's Shadow: The Hidden Power of Feline Magick

The Bastet Codex: Unlocking the Goddess's Magickal Secrets

Purring Spells: Harnessing Bastet's Healing Frequencies

Bastet's Nine Lives: Rebirth, Transformation, and Immortality Spells

Primal Currents: Hydrocephalus Magick in the Path of Dino Wicca

The Digital Gold Rush: Mastering E-Commerce and Online Sales

Future Shock: Adapting to the Next Decade of Change

The Quantum Mindset: Think Like a Billionaire

Sacred Motherhood: Awakening the Divine Feminine Within

The Mother's Spellbook: Enchantments for Love, Protection, and Prosperity

The Witch's Guide to Parenting: Raising Empowered and Intuitive Children
The Magick of Motherhood: Reclaiming Your Power Through Rituals
The Pagan Path to Self-Love: A Goddess's Guide to Worth and Confidence
Wild Woman Magick: Unleashing Your Primal Power
The Money Magnet Blueprint: Unlocking Unlimited Wealth
Biohacking 101: Unlock Your Body's Full Potential
The Wild Father: A Pagan Guide to Strength and Wisdom
The Sacred Masculine: Unlocking Your Inner Power
The Druid's Compass
The Warrior's Mindset
The Father's Fire
Odin's Path
Ancestral Bonds
The House That Whispers
The Magician's Code
The Wild Hunt
The Green Man's Path
The Altar of Success
The Shadow and the Sword
The High Priestess's Guide to Energy Healing
The Lunar Mother
The Sacred Self-Care Grimoire
The Womb Wisdom Codex
The Wheel of the Mother
The Witch's Guide to Manifestation
The Q2 Reset
The Ultimate Guide to AI-Powered Passive Income
Escape the 9-5
AI Feline Fortunes
The Tear-Stained Grimoire

Razorblade Runes
Cemetery Sirens
The Midnight Wristwatch
The Town That Forgets
AI Horror & Creepypasta
The Hollow Frequency
The Breach Echo
The Quiet Between Worlds
The Sigil of Tharan-Khul
Summon the Vault of Y'ha'ten
The Becoming Codex
The Profit of Az'ra-nar
The Drowned Logos
Echoes of the Eldritch Will
The Deep Ledger
Necronomicon of Networth
Covenant of the Wealthwyrm
The Whisperer's Manifesto
The Rites of Azh-K'luth
The Ark of the Crawling Coin
The Tithe of Shadows
Inkheart Abyss
The Timewinds of Y'ha-nthlei
The Spiral Labyrinth of Azag-Nirrh
The Gallifreyan Heresy of the Black Pharaoh
The Psalms of Nyog-Sotha
Black Rain Alchemy
The Infinite Maw
The Entropic Blueprint
The Oracle of Sh'guul
The Book of Breach
The Drowned Saint's Testament
Dreamcraft of the Sleeper God

The Silence Market
Cthonomics: The Dark Wealth Algorithm
Invocation of the Ten-Eyed King
Wealthbound to the Wyrm Below
Become the Unnameable
Codex of the Sovereign Flame
Rituals of Relentless Becoming
The Shadow Ascends
The Eyes Beneath You
The Will That Wakes Worlds
Silence Is a Weapon
The Mirror That Screams
The Whisper Between Moments
The Mind That Devours Fear
The Myth of the Finished Self
The Architect of Your Madness
The Voice You've Buried
The Discipline of Madness
Stormborn: Awakening Your Inner Tempest
The Mind That Ate Time
Unbind Your Becoming
The Pact You Owe Yourself
The Devourer's Diet
The Acid That Carves the Path
The Tower You Must Burn
The Breath Between Worlds
Speak Like the Deep
The Labyrinth Within
The Spine of the Sea God
Rejection Is a Portal
The Crown You Refused
The Scar Is the Spell
The Lightless Flame

The Habit of Becoming Horrific
ChickenJockey Chaos
The Gatekeeper Within
You Are Not Your Name
The Compass of the Mad
The Archive of Unsent Letters
What the Mirror Can't Show You
The Knife You Needed
Worship Nothing, Become Everything
The Other Voice
The Body the World Forgot
The Vein of the Void
The Black Bone Codex
The Puzzle of the Hidden Self (Millennium Puzzle)
The Eye That Sees the Lie *(Millennium Eye)*
The Ring of Return (Millennium Ring)
The Rod of Relentless Will *(Millennium Rod)*
The Tally of the Soul (Millennium Tauk/Necklace)
The Key to the Locked Timeline (Millennium Key)
The Scale of Sacred Decisions (Millennium Scales)
Inferno Bites: The UnOfficial Minecraft Lava Cookbook
Rot in the Attic
Prana: The Hidden Force of Your Infinite Self
The Shadow Realm Within: Transforming Darkness Into Destiny
The Borderland Collapse
Claws of Protection: Bastet's Defensive Magick
Mr. Ring-a-Ding's Madness
Yugioh Astrology: Celestial Deckcraft and Duel Destiny (2026–2027 Edition)
The Seal You Signed: Unlocking the Power You Once Feared
The Puzzle of Infinite Minds: Unlocking the Mentalism Hidden Within

The Eye That Mirrors the All: Secrets of Inner Reflection
Doctor Who: The Toymaker's Broadcast
The Rod of Eternal Flow: Commanding the Currents of Vibration
Golden Eyes of Bastet: Enhancing Psychic Vision
The Key of Dual Forces: Balance Within the Polarity
The Scales of Living Rhythm: Timing the Dance of Life
The Necklace of Hidden Cause: Weaving the Webs of Fate
The Ring of Secret Masters: Rising Through the All Within All
Daggers of the Dying Deep
Bastet's Wealth and Fortune Magick: Prosperity Rituals of the Goddess
The Tide that Speaks
The Scrolls of Petosiris: 13 Rituals from the Feathered Eye
Petosiris and the Living Plague of Osirion
Feline Fire: Bastet's Passion and Love Magick
The Star Altar of Petosiris
Bastet's Whiskers: Supernatural Sensory Magick
The Bastet Grimoire
Feeding the Shadows
The Mouthless Prayer
The Spiral Wound
Becoming the Ibis: Lessons from Petosiris's Mind
The Crimson Coven: Cola Magick for Sweet Dominion
Sacred Cat's Paw
The Soda Zodiac: A Flavor for Every Sign
Covenant of the Crawling Flame
The Ink of Ish'Zur
Frothroot: The Thirst That Ate the World
The Golden Glyphs of Prosperity
The Etherbind Codex
Echoes of the Resistance: Reclaiming the You That Survived

Harnessed Minds: Breaking Free from Mental Control
The Eyes in the Smoke
Rootwake: The Carbon Covenant
Skitter Logic: Unlearning the Fear That Built You
Doctor Who: The World That Froths
Rootwake: The Fizz That Rewrites Flesh
Rootwake: Frothfather of the World
The Holly Pact: Blood Beneath the Mistletoe
The 2nd Mass Principle: Building Unbreakable Tribes
Web of Wits: A Survival Guide to Encounters with Anasi the Spider (Aunt Nancy)
The Hexbreaking Handbook: Effective Spells to Remove Curses
Pop Alchemy: Transform Your Life One Sip at a Time
The Mason Code: Leading in Unleadable Times
Petosiris and the Fifth Chamber of Thoth
The Ether Seed Within
The Parent of Tomorrow
Petosiris's Pyramid of Perpetual Wealth
Unlearn the World
Grimoire of the Hollow Tongue
Zodiac Weeds: Finding Your Strain Through the Stars
Aquarius Rises in the Bank
The Sugar God's Smile
The Skinclock Reversal: Biohacking the Face of Time
Debtburn: How to Obliterate What You Owe Forever
The Ice Cream Oracle: What Your Cone Says About Your Future
Silence Is Sovereignty: The Power of Being Unreadable
The Wind That Whispers Through Stone
Path of the Four Directions
Doctor Who: The Maestro's Symphony of Endings
Oxygen Grail: Breathing to Undo the Clock

Zodiacal Collapse: When Stars Devour Time

Teachings from the Red Sand Silence

Doctor Who: Omega – The Broken Equation

Memory Wipe Your Past: Start Over Like a MiB

Mitochondria Prime: Ignite the Core of Youth

A Nest of Roaches

Grub from the Galaxy: MiB Recipes You'll Never Forget

Whiskers of Power: Bastet's Guide to Inner Sovereignty

The Gift Must Cost Them: Negotiation Through Unequal Exchange

The Worm Guys' Wealth Code: Hustle Like an Alien

Bug Out: The Edgar Method for Ruthless Goal Setting

Weaving Life with Spiderwoman's Pattern

Doctor Who: The Rani's Renaissance

How to Get a Job (If You're a Puppygirl)

Speak Through Others: The Art of Proxy Power

T-Rex Your Trauma: Reclaim the Power of Your Primal Self

The Black Briefcase: How MiB Stay Wealthy in Silence

The Thirst Beyond Reason: Understanding Diabetes Insipidus From the Inside Out

Backwoods Witchcraft for Billionaires: The Pagan Path from Dirt Roads to Gold Roads

The Moonshine Grimoire: Fermented Spells for Abundance

The Nameless Geometry

The Wraith's Mixtape: Spellcasting with Songs of Sorrow

The Gallifreyan Gentleman: Silent Wealth, Sonic Confidence, and the Doctor's Code of Living

Sugar Water Confidence

Dino Totems: Spirit Guides from Earth's First Gods

Pumpkin Sigils & Ritual Smoke

The Hózhó Compass

The Distortus Discipline – Order from Inner Mutation

Witchcraft for the Cold-Blooded Soul

S'mores of the Damned: Haunted Recipes for Halloween Night

Rethink the Drink: A Beverage Survival Guide for DI Warriors

The Shadow Chord: Guitar Magick and Sonic

Malformed Yet Majestic: Leading When You Feel Wrong Inside

The Cursed Diary: Ink-Stained Spells of the Emo Soul

Anxiety Off Switch: Emergency Reset for a Fried Nervous System

The Energy Heist: How to Take Back Your Life from Drainers

Beyond the Bathroom: Rebuilding Your Social Life With DI

Coyote's Gift for Decision Makers

Ghoul-Goo: Spooky S'mores You'll Die For

Echoes in the Mirror: Scrying and Self-Destruction Magick

Thread and Thorn: Stitching Spells from Rural Cloth

The Mogwai Mind: Building Untouchable Wealth from Small Ideas

Be Your Own Guide: Trust Your Inner Compass

Hormones in Chaos: The Endocrine Puzzle of Diabetes Insipidus

ChronoCleanse: Detox Your Biological Timeline

The Limb You Hide Is the One That Saves You

Leaves, Bones, and Whisper Spells

The Dinosaur Mindset: Prehistoric Tactics for Modern Wealth

Clawing Back Control: A Bastet Method for Boundaries and Empowerment

Samhain Codes of the Forgotten

Orange Alchemy: The Autumnal Spellbook

Monster Within, Master Without

The Sigil That Sleeps

Hearthcraft: Yule Hearth Sigils and Winter Warmth Spells

Temple of the Purring Moon: Rituals from Bastet's Lineage
When the Earth Remembers Your Footsteps
Food for Mood: Eat to Heal Depression, Not Just Survive It
Witch of the Kudzu Vine: Southern Pagan Wealth Secrets
The Invisible Diagnosis: Advocating for Yourself With DI
The Coffin's Lullaby: Sleep Magick and Nightmares as Portals
Ashes of the Will: Rituals for Erasing the Self
The Fracture Rite: Shattering the Magickal Core
Funeral Candles: The Art of Emo Flame Magick
The Black Grimoire: A Blank Ritual for Writing in Absence
Phantom Thirst: A Halloween Survival Guide for Diabetes Insipidus
The Hollow Crown: Emo Royalty and Magick of the Outcast King
Sandpainting for the Soul
Falling Into Balance: Using the Extra Hour to Recalibrate Life
100 Southern Superstitions That Still Work
The DI Child: A Parent's Guide to Raising Hydrated, Happy Kids
The Jungle of Shame: Escaping the Hidden Lab of Doubt
The Witch's Toast: S'mores Spells and Creepy Confections
The Hoodoo Pantry: Spells from the Mason Jar
The Immortal Fortune: Secret Wealth Lessons from Captain Jack Harkness
The Specter's Embrace: Magick for Channeling Ghostly Lovers
Grateful Waters: A Thanksgiving Survival Guide for Diabetes Insipidus
The Seizure Gospel
Harvestbind: Autumn Sigils and Samhain Spells
Doctor Who: The Algorithmic Awakening
Silent Nights, Steady Waters: A Christmas Survival Guide for Diabetes Insipidus

The Extra Hour Effect: How One Hour Can Transform Everything

Blade Between the Breaths

Running with the Mountain Shadows

Echoes of the Failed Experiment – Becoming a Living Legacy

Swamp Witches & River Ghosts: Real Southern Hauntings

Cornbread Prophecies: Magical Recipes from a Southern Table

Doctor Who: The Signal in the Star

Bloomcraft: Spring Sigils and Equinox Enchantments

Vanisher: How to Disappear from the Internet Without Losing Your Life

The Ultimate Christmas Cookie Cookbook

The Unbreakable Parent: How to Mentally Survive Raising Kids in a Broken World

Time Debt: How to Reclaim the Hours You Didn't Know You Lost

One Month, One Million: Unconventional Cash Creation Tactics

Doctor Who: The Cyber Conversion Protocol

Black Friday Frenzy: The Art of Finding Hidden Online Deals

The Grimoire Buried Under the Apple Tree

Digital Couponing Masterclass: Your Step-by-Step Guide to Black Friday Savings

The Fire Inside the Flint

Shadows on the Ceiling: The Emo Guide to Astral Magick

The Bone-Eaters Beneath Us

Black Friday Bundle Blueprint: Creating Irresistible Product Packages for Maximum Sales

Thirteen Nights of Unbinding

Doctor Who: Engines of Influence

Pumpkin Spice Alchemy: Recipes of Fire and Frost

When Raptor Met Rexy: Prehistoric Lessons in Wild Romance
Oblivion's Candle: Burn the Path Behind You
Campfire Curses and Chocolate: A Halloween S'mores Grimoire
The Wallet That Wasn't Mine: Breaking Free from Inherited Scarcity
The Cola Zodiac: What Your Fizz Says About Your Fate
Frostfire Fortune: Unlocking Winter's Hidden Prosperity
Signal Jamming: Detox Your Brain from Info Overload
The Dust of the Forgotten Rite
The Golden Cat Sigils: Drawing Power in Bastet's Name
Mud Magick: The Prosperity of Getting Dirty
Savory Spicefall: Beyond the Pumpkin Pie
Pumpkin Spice Apothecary Kitchen
The Pumpkin Spice Economy: Turning Trends into Billions
The Ember Veil: 13 Nights of Fire Magick
Financial Freeze: When Earning Triggers Panic
The Gingerbread Alchemist: Sweet Recipes with a Twist
Biosynth Power: Programming Yourself from Scratch
Echoes from the Talking Circle
Truffle Alchemy: Fungus of Fortune
Spores of Power: The Truffle Witch's Handbook
Doctor Who: The Tower That Speaks
The Mycelium Veil: Truffle Magick Unbound
Broke But Ashamed: Healing the Shame Wound of Debt
The Evergreen Mind: Growth Through Winter Stillness
The Black Veil Truffle Rite
The Voice Beneath Symbols
Witchlight on the Bayou: Swamp Spells for Sovereignty
I Grew Up Poor and Now I Sabotage My Success
The Lantern of Hollow Souls

Shutdown Survival: A Citizen's Guide to Thriving When Government Stops

When Abundance Feels Like a Threat: Healing the Hidden Fears of Enough

The Scarecrow Grimoire

Owls of the October Veil

Candlewax and Curses: A Halloween Spellbook

Excavating the Inner Fossil – Transforming Fossilized Thoughtforms into Tools of Power

The Yule Witch's Spellbook: Magick for the Holiday Season

Haunted Christmas: Ghost Stories for Winter Nights

The Christmas Survival Guide: Thriving Through the Chaos

The Bone Orchard Rites

Haunted Commerce: The Ghost in the Marketplace

When Money Triggers the Inner Child

Silent Night with the Silence: A Christmas Thriller

The Lightning Crown: Living and Leading Through Seizures

TARDIS Tidings: Festive Stories from the Whoniverse

Autumn Reset: Slowing Down Without Falling Behind

The Trillion Dollar Soul: Rewriting the Currency of Reality

Truffle Eclipse Magick

Micro-Manifestations: Quick Magick That Works

5-Minute Rituals for Busy Witches

The Marshmallow Massacre: Halloween Treats with a Sinister Twist

Blood and Blackberry Thorns

Magickal Mornings: Rituals for a Blessed Christmas Day

Embers of the All-Hallows Fire

The Pumpkin Market Collapse

The Hour You Gained: Transforming Time Into Power

The Chamber Must Be Sealed: Mastering the Power of Controlled Access

The Cursed Manuscript of Petosiris

10 Secrets to Surviving Holiday Crowds
The Witch's Dow Jones
The Witches' Graveyard Shift
Pumpkin Sigils: Carving Rites for Midnight Power
The Secret Shopper's Black Friday Guide: How to Get Early Access and VIP Deals
Fever in the Foundation
The Neuralyzer Reset: Reprogram Your Morning Routine
Lightning Lessons of the White Painted Woman
The Enchanted Snowflake
The Magic Sip: Surviving Disney Parks with Diabetes Insipidus
The One Who Draws Through You
Santa's Secrets: A Magical Holiday Planner
Silent Bells, Loud Miracles: Self-Help for the Season of Stillness
The Sugar Spell Codex: Confectionary Magick of Christmas
Autumn Hexcraft: Fallen Leaves, Fallen Barriers
Sleep Like a Fortress: Build a Life Where Insomnia Can't Survive
Nowhere Was Ever Home
Christmas Under the Stars: A Celestial Holiday Guide
Rentproof: How to Never Be Evicted Again
Workless: Escape the 9-5 Without Being Broke
The Gilded Gift: A Wealth Altar for Christmas Morning
The Black Friday Grimoire
The Hollowing: Ceremonies of Spiritual Collapse
Doctor Who: The Nameless Signal
Where the Eagle Hides His Courage
The Dwarf Tyrant's Ascent: Claiming Power in a World of Giants
The Currency of the Dead: Trading with Spectral Bankers
The Icebound Witch: Survival and Magick in the Cold

The Emergency Money Mind: Constant Crisis, Zero Calm

Thirst & Roses: A Valentine's Survival Guide for Diabetes Insipidus

Springing Into Clarity: Mastering the Energy Shift of Daylight Saving

Speed of the Nanotyrant: Agile Strategies for Life's Hunt

The 90-Day Reset: A Science-Backed Guide to Reinvent Yourself Before the New Year

The Coil of Thorns

Timegates Unleashed

Dopamine Fasting 2.0: Rewiring Your Brain in a World of Overstimulation

The Nanotyrannus Mutation: Embracing Your Differentiated Form

Unwritten January: How to Use the Blank Page of the Year to Re-Author Your Life

Feast of the Forgotten Spirits: Ancestor Magick for the Holidays

The Burnout Codex: A System for Thriving Beyond Stress

I Don't Deserve to Have Money

When the King Doesn't See You: The Shadow Predator's Guide

The Reset Ritual :A Guide to Shedding Last Year's Weight—Emotional and Physical—by Spring Cleaning Your Soul

Calendar Alchemy: Learn to Bend Time and Productivity around Your Natural Rhythms

The Mirror Contract: A One-Sentence Agreement with Yourself that Unlocks Real Change

The Nile Formula: Sacred Flow for Millionaire Minds

Forward Momentum: Productivity Rituals for the Lost Hour

Harvest Gold: Wealth Magick of Pumpkin Spice Commerce

The Magick of Christmas Lights: Illuminating Holiday Rituals

Cranberry Crown: Royal Self-Worth through Ritual Meals
Petosiris and the Worms of the Feathered Throne
The Evergreen Equation: Self-Help for Sustained Growth
The Rain Will Wash Us Away: Emo Weather Magick
Snowlight Shadows: Magick Under Frozen Stars
Doctor Who: Merger of Empires
The Light Within the Feast: Magickal Wealth of Yuletide Flame
Momentum Machines: Small Habits Designed to Snowball into Unstoppable Forward Motion
Calm Spells: Magickal Solutions for Anxiety Relief
Santa's Final List: The Naughty Never Leave
The Mystic's Guide to Banishing Worry
The Silence Dividend: Turning Quiet Mornings into Compounding Growth All Year
Charmed Stillness: Rituals to Ease the Mind
Blood Spiral Ascension
The Vanishing Heart Invocation
Crystal Calm: Harnessing Stones for Anxiety
The Nano Tyrant Code: Strength in the Small Predator
The Energy Ledger: Accounting Methods for Vitality, Not Just Money
Snowglobe Mindset: Shake Up Your Thoughts, Settle Into Peace
The Weight of the Feather: Anubis's Codes for Soul Balance
Pocket Peppermint Power: Tiny Rituals for Big Holiday Energy
Shadowkeeper of the Golden Jackal: Anubis's Path to Energetic Protection
The Witch's Breath: Anxiety Relief Through Magickal Breathing
The Tiny Ember: Pocket Motivation for Cold Days

Stocking Sorcery: Mini Spells for Holiday Luck and Prosperity

Warm Hands, Steady Heart: Micro Grounding for Winter Anxiety

The Jackal's Lantern: Guide-Lights for Walking the Dark Path

Anubis's Silent Steps: Rituals for Stealth, Peace & Emotional Quiet

The Bonewake Protocol

Extinction-Proof: How to Outlive Trends, Trauma, and Time

The Fourth Doctor: The Eccentric Wanderer

The Second Doctor: Chaos and Charm in the TARDIS (Patrick Troughton, 1966–1969)

The Third Doctor: Earthbound Defender of Time (Jon Pertwee, 1970–1974)

The First Doctor: Genesis of the Time Lord (William Hartnell, 1963–1966)

The Fourth Doctor: The Eccentric Wanderer *(Tom Baker, 1974–1981)*

The Fifth Doctor: Elegance and Empathy (Peter Davison, 1982–1984)

The Sixth Doctor: A Kaleidoscope of Conflict (Colin Baker, 1984–1986)

The Seventh Doctor: The Strategist of Shadows (Sylvester McCoy, 1987–1989)

The Eighth Doctor: A Time Lord's Renaissance (Paul McGann, 1996)

The War Doctor: A Time Lord's Burden (John Hurt, 2013)

The Ninth Doctor: The Healer of Worlds
(Christopher Eccleston, 2005)

The Tenth Doctor: The Lonely Hero (David Tennant, 2005–2010)

The Eleventh Doctor: The Madman in a Box (Matt Smith, 2010–2013)

The Twelfth Doctor: The Rebel with a Cause (Peter Capaldi, 2013–2017)

The Thirteenth Doctor: Breaking the Mold
(Jodie Whittaker, 2017–2022)

The Fourteenth Doctor: A New Beginning (David Tennant, 2022–2023)

The Fifteenth Doctor: Rewriting the Stars
(Ncuti Gatwa, 2023–2025)

Santa's Shortcut to Success: Micro Habits for a Better New Year

The Midnight Cocoa Manifesto: Comfort Rituals for Hard Nights

Why I Can't Save: Trauma Blocks to Financial Planning

Dino Brain, Mega Goals: Rewire Yourself for Savage Success.

Jurassic Profit: Unearth Your Inner Millionaire Fossil

Scales & Softness: Dating with Dino Heart

Carnotaurus Dreams.

Red Willow Thinking.

Reindeer Resilience: How to Keep Going When You're Exhausted

Candlewick Courage: Lighting Strength in Dark Seasons.

Elf-Mode Focus: Fast Attention Fixes for Busy Seasons

Futureproof Feelings – Emotional Skill-Building for Resilience No Matter What the New Year Brings

Get Some Tarot cards: https://www.makeplayingcards.com/sell/apophis-occult-shop

Get some shirts: https://www.bonfire.com/store/apophis-shirt-emporium/

Instagrams:
@apophis_enterprises,
@apophisbookemporium,
@apophisscardshop
Twitter: @apophisenterpr1
Tiktok:@apophisenterprise
Youtube: @sg1fan23477
Hive: @sg1fan23477
CheeLee: @SG1fan23477

Podcast: Apophis Chat Zone: https://open.spotify.com/show/5zXbrCLEV2xzCp8ybrfHsk?si=fb4d4fdbdce44dec

Newsletter: https://apophiss-newsletter-27c897.beehiiv.com/

If you want to support me or see posts of other projects that I have come over to: **buymeacoffee.com/mpetchinskg**

I post there daily several times a day

Get your Dinowicca or Christmas themed digital products, especially Santa Raptor songs and other musics. Here: **https://sg1fan23477.gumroad.com**

Apophis Yuletide Digital has not only digital Christmas items, but it will have all things with Dinowicca as well as other Digital products.

www.ingramcontent.com/pod-product-compliance
Lightning Source LLC
LaVergne TN
LVHW022230200926
848481LV00006B/2201
* 9 7 9 8 2 9 5 4 5 1 5 8 4 *